Grow Your Business

Grow Your
Business

*How to build a world-class business
one relationship at a time*

Matt Bird

Matador
9 Priory Business Park,
Wistow Road, Kibworth Beauchamp,
Leicestershire. LE8 0RX
Tel: 0116 279 2299
Email: books@troubador.co.uk
Web: www.troubador.co.uk/matador
Twitter: @matadorbooks

ISBN 978 1789015 768
British Library Cataloguing in Publication Data.
A catalogue record for this book is available from the British Library.

Printed and bound in the UK by TJ International, Padstow, Cornwall
Typeset in 11pt Aldine by Troubador Publishing Ltd, Leicester, UK

Matador is an imprint of Troubador Publishing Ltd

To my wife Esther, and children, Joseph, Matilda and Reuben, from whom I learn most about relationships.

What business leaders say...

"*Matt has distilled the key aspects of relationship-building and commercial know-how into a single book that focuses on growing a business. A must-read!*"
Richard Oldfield, Global Markets Leader for PwC

"*If you want to grow your business, I strongly recommend you read this book. Matt provides practical strategies you can action immediately to achieve results.*"
Sir Peter Vardy, Chairman of Vardy Group

"*As readable as ever, Matt's new book is full of practical advice that is accessible, easy to implement and could radically grow your business. I have always found Matt's desire to help others and share best practice to be an inspiration, and found his advice effective and based on a deep respect and understanding of others.*"
Robert Hughes-Penney, Investment Director at Rathbones

"*Matt Bird is one of those rare breeds of individuals who seems to make things happen when you think the chances of pulling it off is perhaps no more than 10 per cent. He is tenacious and doesn't take no for an answer. Determination, in my opinion, is one of the key ingredients of any successful person.*"
Lord Bob Edmiston, Chairman of IM Group

"In Relationology 101, Matt Bird powerfully made the case for building strong relationships. Here he takes us to the next level, demystifying the strategies and giving insights that will help you to develop those relationships and grow your business."
Darren Mitchell, Global Deputy COO at Hogan Lovell

"Matt Bird has written his best book yet, one which I'd recommend as an indispensable tool to keep you on track as you grow your business."
Simon Hickman, CEO of Access Insurance

"Whilst corporate success is ultimately defined by the financial results, "people" are the engine which powers business to grow. When there are relationships that acknowledge competence, place a high focus on respect and focus on the development of team rather than superstar qualities, the chances of success are greatly enhanced. This book has so many implementable lessons which I'm hoping to take forward in our businesses."
Terry Rosenberg, Chair of Multiply Group

"Authentic, purposeful relationships are rarely accidental and in business they really matter. Matt offers a framework and tested practices to help us all invest in people and cultivate the mutually beneficial relationships that help people and organisations thrive."
John Cotterell, Chief Executive of Endava

"One of the most important needs of any human being is connectivity with other people, even more so in this ever changing, digitalised world we currently live in. Matt Bird clearly understands that real, authentic relationships are becoming increasingly important to experience business success in this new economic landscape."
Kobus Nel, CEO of Fairtree Capital

"Look deeply into your business and you will see relationships at the heart of it, Matt Bird is the Sherpa who can guide you to make those relationships great!"
Paul Jackson OBE, CEO of Dovetail Games

"As a human resource practitioner, I have learnt that even though a cliche, it is true that the biggest asset any company has are its people. Managing a company's biggest asset can be complicated; and the ability to do so with success requires a special skill which Matt talks about so expertly. The world of work is fortunate to have this book on how to develop relationships - the real secret on how to grow any business."
Dr Ellen Hagan, CEO of L'aine Services

"Matt Bird brings his usual deep insights about human nature towards building and maintaining productive commercial relationships to his new book Grow Your Business. The book is a MUST READ for anyone in business."
Cyrus Pardiwala, PwC International

Contents

Contents

Introduction

Grow Your Business is more than a book, workbook and masterclass programme; it is a unique business growth system to enable you to create, maintain and grow a world-class relational ecosystem of your own.

The quality of your relationships determines your quality of life. As President Theodore Roosevelt said, "The most important single ingredient in the formula of success is knowing how to get on with people." Whatever business success looks like for you, the greatest factor contributing to your achievement is your relational ecosystem.

Relationships improve your career possibilities and opportunities. As we shall explore later, the majority of jobs are, in fact, never advertised, but rather offered through existing relationships. So when it comes to securing a new job or client, do you want to have greater choice by fishing in the majority pool or less choice from the minority pool?

Relationships improve your efficiency and performance. Trusting relationships are the fastest, simplest and easiest way to get anything done. As Chris du Toit, a Private Equity Fund Executive from Multiply Group, explains, "A business can only grow to the degree of trust that exists within it."

The focus of this book is to help you develop the mindset, skills and behaviours you need to build a powerful relational ecosystem in order to have the maximum impact on your career development, team performance and business growth. However, there are some other significant benefits that you will gain on the way.

I have observed the additional impact that relationships have upon health and well-being. I hadn't realised their significance until I researched this idea for a keynote speech I was giving at a public health conference and came across the *Harvard Study of Adult Development*. The *Harvard Study of Adult Development* is the longest longitudinal study in history, spanning eight decades and now with its fourth director of studies.

The study has followed the development of hundreds of men. The third director of studies, Professor George Vaillant, concluded his research saying, 'Happiness is love!' The fourth director of studies, Professor Robert Waldinger, wrote that, 'The quality of your relationships at the age of 50 years old determines the quality of your health at the age of 80 years old.'

Professor Julianne Holt-Lunstad of Brigham Young University published a research paper, *Social Relationships and Mortality Risk*, in which she said of her study group that there was 'a 50% increased likelihood of survival for participants with stronger social relationships'. She concluded her research explaining, 'The influence of social relationships on risk for mortality is comparable with well-established risk factors for mortality, such as smoking.'

So, not only do the quality of our relationships determine business growth and performance, but they also have an extraordinary effect on human happiness, health and longevity of life. Relationships are just too important to leave to chance.

One of the most important things we can do in life and business is to create, curate and capitalise on our relational ecosystem. The *Grow Your Business* book, workbook and masterclass programme offer a way for you to become intentional about creating, maintaining and growing a relational ecosystem that will ensure your success.

Matt Bird

mattbird@relationology.co.uk
www.relationology.co.uk
www.facebook.com/relationology
www.twitter.com/relationology
www.instagram.com/relationology
www.youtube.com/relationologytv

Create Your Relational Ecosystem

The first priority in building your relational ecosystem is to be intentional about creating new relationships. You may have been collecting relationships all your life or you may have become awakened to their importance later on; whichever, it is never too late to start and you certainly should never stop.

It is vital to realise that you cannot rush the process when it comes to creating new relationships; they happen one at a time. Professor Alberto-Laszlo Barabasi of the Central European University has done extensive research into social networks and he has created two general concepts as a result. The first concept revolves around the idea of growth – that the number of people in a social network increases one person at a time. The second concept revolves around preferential attachment – the idea that the more relationships a person has, the more likely they are to attract other relationships. Neither theory is rocket science; however, the growth concept of adding one person at a time is extremely practical.

For the majority of people, the thought of walking into a crowded room full of strangers is rather uncomfortable. The idea of having to 'network' and talk to lots of people you don't know and then have hundreds of business cards thrust upon you with the expectation you'll do something with them isn't a pleasant one. But the reality is you don't have to. Your relational ecosystem will grow over time, so you don't need to worry about engineering opportunities to meet lots of people and make lots of meaningful conversation. Instead, you can patiently build your relational ecosystem on an incremental basis.

So, take the pressure off. Forget trying to meet lots of new people in the shortest time possible and instead focus on one. When you go to a business conference, seminar or drinks reception, remind yourself that whilst you might talk with lots of people, you are looking for one person who you can have a meaningful connection with and then add to your ecosystem.

The first section of this book explores five keys that will enable you to become world-class at building your relational ecosystem one person at a time.

Key 1. Go Out and Win New Business Today

One day, the owner of an agency that makes short films for businesses was working at home. He was in the midst of a project, with his laptop and paperwork spread across the dining room table, when Mother Nature called. So, he headed to the toilet. As he sat there, he reached out to the shelf of magazines put there for just such an occasion and picked up the publication at the top of the pile. The magazine was for a clothing brand. As he flicked through the pages, he was impressed with what he saw. What went through his mind was, 'If they can do this on paper, imagine what they could do on film!'

When he returned to the dining room table, he googled the name of the Chief Executive of the business, found their email and sent them a message. The gist of his email went something like this: 'Dear X, I was just sat on the toilet looking at your brochure and thought, 'Woh, if you could do this on paper, imagine what you could do on film.'' He then went on to describe his film-making services. When he was done, he pressed the send button in hopeful anticipation. Within a couple of days, he heard back. The Chief Executive wanted to meet him. As a result, his business began making induction films for new employees and films for the company website. If only the search for new clients was always so successful and profitable.

The Power of Asking

There is some ancient wisdom that says, 'Ask and you will receive, seek and you will find, knock and the door will be opened to you.' Winning new business often comes down to having the courage to ask. It may be a completely cold call, like the story of the film-maker previously; a referral from a current client; or an intermediary asking who they can refer to you at this time.

The reason many businesses don't grow is because they have forgotten about the power of a simple ask. If we asked the right people the right questions, we would have a better opportunity of winning the right work. I will now explore five relational strategies for winning new business through the power of asking.

Strategy 1: Self-introduction

A few years ago, I read an interview in a newspaper with the incoming Chief Executive of a UK high-street bank. I immediately thought that this was someone I would like to meet, so I crafted a letter of introduction inviting him for a drink after work. It was a bit of a long shot given I was the owner of a boutique business and he was a global banking executive. In the newspaper interview, he mentioned an area of interest that we shared, so I included mention of that in the introductory letter. Within a week of sending my letter, I received a personal reply inviting me to contact his diary secretary to make an appointment. We met, got on and have done various things together ever since.

This business development strategy is what I call the 'self-introduction'. It has a high risk of failure – chances are you won't receive a reply at all, or you'll get a polite response declining your services. There is an outside chance that you may be referred to someone else within the organisation. The key to a successful self-introduction, as indicated in my story, is to find some common ground, whether personal or professional, that might pique the interest of the recipient.

Now, for every story of successful self-introduction, I can tell you at least another ten unsuccessful ones. It's a high-risk strategy in the sense that there is a high likelihood of rejection. However, all it costs is the time taken for a thoughtful telephone call or a carefully crafted letter, or approaching the person at an event. The worst a person can say is no!

Strategy 2: Facilitated Introduction

A year ago I met three businessmen in a country I had never been to before. For a number of reasons, I would be visiting there on a regular basis and so I naturally wanted to do some business within the country. I asked one of the businessmen if there were any senior executives in the banking and professional services sector that he could introduce me to. As a complete stranger in the city and country, I knew it would be extremely difficult to introduce myself. The gentleman introduced me to seven people by email. In advance of my visit, I secured meetings with four of them and two of them immediately engaged my services. This is the power of a facilitated introduction.

The facilitated introduction has a lower risk of failure than self-introduction because of what I call 'trust transfer'. A trust transfer takes place between the introducer to the introduced, so the third party is far more likely to accept the invitation to meet. An element of risk is reduced because there is an established relationship of trust that already exists. The trust transfer might be made through a three-way meal, an email or simply permission to use the introducer's name when contacting a particular individual. The way the introduction is made carries different levels of trust transfer, with a three-way face-to-face meeting having a higher level than just an email introduction.

In a facilitated introduction, the introducer shoulders much of the risk. Making trust transfers is like an investment where your deposit can go down as well as up. If the person you introduce does well by the person they are introduced to, then their trust in you grows. If, however, the opposite happens and the person you introduce treats the person they are introduced to badly, then their trust in you diminishes. Trust is a currency whose value can go up or down and it's certainly not something that can be invested lightly.

There is an African proverb that says, 'A friend of a friend is a friend.' This means that if someone *you* are in a trusting relationship with introduces you to someone *they* are in a trusting relationship with, you should offer the person the same privileges.

Strategy 3: Client Recommendation

The third business development strategy is client recommendation. This is about doing such a good job for your clients that they spread the value of your services by word of mouth. Recently, I delivered a Relationology Masterclass on business development for an investment management business and the feedback rippled all the way back to the Chief Executive and Human Resource Director. Before I knew what had happened, I was being rebooked to deliver the training to multiple other offices around the UK. This is the power of client recommendation.

This approach can be proactive as well as reactive, because you ask a client if there is anyone they could recommend you to. The phrase that I often use with clients is, "Is there anyone you think I should be talking to at the moment?" It is a deliberately non-directive, low-pressure and unthreatening question. It is easy for the client to say, "No one comes to mind," but in my experience, more often than not, they name someone – sometimes several people.

As they describe the profile of the person they'd like to recommend you to, you can make your own judgement about whether they are someone you would like to connect with. If they are, you can follow with, "Do you know them very well?" You can then ask, "Would you be happy to recommend me to them?" At that point, they will decide how much trust transfer they are willing to invest; is it simply a name, an email introduction or a lunch together?

The client recommendation is one of the main ways I build out my relational ecosystem, especially internationally.

Strategy 4: Professional Referral

One evening, I was having dinner with a friend at one of London's most iconic buildings. The chef came out to say hello and we got on to talking about changes he wanted to make to the menu. He mentioned that they only had a single cheese variety available at any time and that he was interested in adding a cheese plate selection. I have a small interest in Buchanan's Cheesemongers, which provide artisan cheeses to London's top restaurants, and so I offered to make a referral, which was welcomed. As a result, the restaurant now offers a cheese plate selection provided by Buchanan's cheesemongers.

This is the business development strategy known as the 'professional referral'. What is unique about a referral is that it is made at the point of need – when someone is in need of a particular product or service at a particular time. This relies on your having a relational ecosystem of not only people that you know, but, more importantly, people that know you and know what you do.

For many people working in the financial and professional services sector, building a network of intermediaries who can make professional referrals is their main approach to business development. For a trusted advisor, building intermediary relationships is a relatively unthreatening thing to do because they are fundamentally building relationships with people like them. For example, investment directors will build relationships with independent financial advisors, lawyers and accountants, so that when their clients need investment advice they become their first point of call.

There is a trust transfer at work in professional referrals. If an Independent Financial Advisor (IFA) refers an investment director to a client and they deliver a good financial return, then trust in the IFA grows. However, if they don't, trust in the IFA goes down. So, professional referrers have got a lot to lose as well as a lot to gain. There is a trust bank in each of our relationships from which we need to ensure that we make frequent deposits and fewer withdrawals, and certainly none that make us overdrawn!

Strategy 5: Brand Advocate

Apple has developed an extremely strong community of loyal users who believe that their devices and operating systems are superior to any other. All over the world, Apple users are constantly trying to persuade PC users to move over to Apple because it is better. These customers are not paid to persuade the world that Apple is best, but they do it because they have become brand advocates.

I can remember the first time someone told me about a private car hire service that you could order from an app on your smartphone at half the price of a traditional taxi. My friend was so passionate about the service they had recently discovered, that I couldn't resist trying it. As a result, I became an early adopter of Uber and now use it all over the world.

Despite some minor downsides, I love the service and have become a brand advocate for them too.

Creating a powerful brand experience, like those constructed by Apple and Uber, is not fast, easy or cheap. It does, however, create brand advocates who generate prospective customers and clients for the business, often without any financial incentive.

We will explore how you build a personal and corporate brand in 'Key 3: Attract a Constant Stream of New Business'.

Pre-qualified Leads

One of the benefits of these five relational strategies is that each of them provides pre-qualified leads into your relational ecosystem. They are not random inbound enquiries from a marketing campaign where each lead needs to be filtered and qualified. Instead, each person that is introduced, recommended or referred is done so by someone with real knowledge of you and your business.

Each of the five strategies is powerful in their own right. However, they are at their most powerful when they are used as part of a toolkit that you can draw from as circumstances require. They range from low cost-options, like the self-introduction, through to the high-cost option of building a community of brand advocates. The effectiveness and level of risk attached to each also varies. For example, in self-introduction, you have a high risk of being rejected whereas if you can nurture brand advocates, you will have a very low risk of being turned away.

People often want a formula to help them decide which approach to choose, but it all comes down to personal discernment. Knowing which approach to use is often a matter of following your gut instinct based on the live feedback that people are giving you. This is all grounded in knowledge that you build up through experience and good, old-fashioned trial and error.

Key 2. Maximise Your Existing Client Portfolio

There is no denying that going out and winning new business requires an enormous amount of time, energy and resources. Along the way, there will be setbacks that will knock your confidence and from which you will need to find the inner resources to bounce back. Finding new business is often referred to as 'hunting' because it is about getting out into the wilds of the marketplace and looking for your next meal. Hunting has a high cost of client acquisition and is often led by people who tend to be highly self-motivated, independent thinkers who can build a breadth of relationships. We covered the various 'hunting' techniques in the previous Key about winning new business.

Another way to grow your business is through 'farming' or expanding your business through current and historic client relationships. This is always a more efficient and effective way to operate. The advantage is you know your clients and they know you, and, assuming you have done a very good job for them, they will already know the value of what you can do for them. In essence, the trust transfer mentioned in Key 1 has already been established. This process is often called farming because it's about caring and nurturing what you have in order to maximise the harvest. Farming, in comparison to hunting, has a low cost in terms of client acquisition and is led by people who tend to be collaborative in style, who gain people's loyalty and build deep relationships.

Morally Dirty Networking

Professor Francesca Gino of Harvard Business School co-authored a study, *The Contaminating Effects of Building Instrumental Ties: How Networking Can Make Us Feel Dirty* (2014). The study concluded, 'Networking makes low-power employees feel unclean, which understandably makes them not want to network. But if they don't network, they may not become high-power employees – who no longer feel dirty when they network.'

The issue at the crux of this is authenticity. People in high-power roles know they can contribute equally to any benefit they may receive from building relationships and so tend to feel authentic about being intentional. In contrast, people in low-power roles feel they have more to gain and less to give. Therefore, they feel networking is 'morally dirty' and inauthentic, and tend to be more hesitant in building relationships as a result.

Key 2 is about how you can grow your relational ecosystem as a result of building out from the relationships you already have. 'Networking' seems daunting for team members and threatening to clients. So, it's simple: let's stop networking and start building relationships. People perceive relationships as something you invest in and expect to see them change and develop over time – it's something we all do quite naturally as part of our everyday lives. Growing your business through relationships is, therefore, something the whole team can be involved in. It isn't the preserve of the few who like networking or sales – it's something for everyone.

In this Key, I am going to look at five strategies for growing your business through farming and maximising existing business relationships.

Strategy 1: Refresh Relationships

In the cut and thrust of business, it is easy to move from one client to the next and the next. As one project comes to an end, you have a celebratory drink or meal, say thank you to everyone involved and move on to the next assignment. This means that client relationships have a tendency to become very transactional and it is not always easy to keep in contact. However, you always have the opportunity to refresh historic client relationships.

In the last week or two of December, I always find that people are trying to get things over the line before the start of the next calendar year. Even if you have planned ahead and been able to get a meeting in the diary, those meetings are often cancelled. So, I've developed the habit of using those weeks to plan my first week back in January. I reach out to all the clients that I've worked with in the previous 12 months and arrange a time to catch up, preferably face-to-face but if not on the telephone. I also include people that I worked with the year before who I've not spoken with much since. This provides an opportunity to refresh relationships and often triggers conversations about how we could work together in the year ahead. The same approach can be used in the run-up to Easter and other significant holiday periods.

It is always best to build relationships before you need them, so people don't feel used and abused. We all have people in our lives who we only ever hear from when they want something from us, and we all know how transactional and grubby that can make our relationships feel. So, the key to refreshing relationships is to do so before you need them. Dropping someone a note to say it would be great to catch up over a coffee couldn't be easier and demonstrates a commitment to building genuine relationships.

Strategy 2: Build Out Relationships

For years, I worked with a partner in a professional services firm and then, one day, he announced he would be retiring in six months time. Of course, I congratulated him and chatted about the next season of his life. Later in the conversation, I said that I'd like to continue working with the firm and wondered if there was a way he could help me build out my relationships within the business. I'm a fine wine and food aficionado and so the partner suggested I host one of my fine wine and artisan cheese tastings, which he could invite a dozen partners to.

He was true to his word and on the evening of the event brought a dozen colleagues who were partners within the firm. We had a fabulous evening, during which I said the briefest of words about Relationology and sent everyone home with a bag of artisan cheese and a copy of one of my books. That evening helped me to build out my relational footprint in the firm and consequently I have continued to work with them. About six months after the event, one of the guests was appointed to the executive board of the firm and asked me to develop a Relationology Masterclass programme to work with a group of partners he was responsible for. The programme was a great success, delivered powerful results for the business and has become my signature programme for other clients ever since.

Strategy 3: Deepen Relationships

It's a great feeling to win a new client and deliver a value-adding piece of work for them. What can be even more satisfying, and mutually beneficial, is to develop a long-term relationship that adds value deep into their business. In order to deepen your relationship in this way, your client needs to know and believe that their success is your success.

In the last years, there are two clients with whom I have done ad hoc pieces of work. They have now asked to retain my services because they believe I am a critical aspect of their business growth. It's incredibly affirming and encouraging when your clients want to build commitment into your value-adding relationship.

When speaking about client relationships, the legendary international motivational speaker Les Brown explains that it isn't our task to achieve customer satisfaction, do a great job or impress people; it is our job to amaze our clients and build deeper relationships with them. This can only be achieved when we under-promise and over-deliver. So think about the extra value that you can offer each and every client you work with.

Strategy 4: Follow Relationships

Over a decade ago, I met a businessman who I kept in contact with from time to time. The first time he asked me to do some work for him, he was with a high-street bank. I had never and, still to this day, have never completed such an arduous due-diligence process. However, it enabled me to win and deliver my Relationology Masterclass programme. Shortly after this, he left the bank and I remember feeling disappointed that a great client relationship was coming to an end, especially considering how long it had taken to establish.

I kept in contact with the gentleman and when he took up a new position with a different firm, he swiftly asked me to do some work with him again. When he transitioned to work for another bank a few years later, guess what? Once he'd got his feet under the table, he called on me again to develop a programme to grow business through relationships across the new business.

What this experience and others like it have taught me is the power of following relationships. When a key contact leaves their job, it actually creates a double opportunity. If you have built out your relationships in the business, you will have other contacts who will engage your services in the same business. Secondly, if you track that person to their new organisation, it creates the possibility of a potential new client.

It's often the small things that are appreciated the most in relationships. When someone announces they are moving on, congratulate them and ask them where they are going.

Suggest that when they have settled in it would be great to catch up and then put a note in your diary to remind you to do so. When someone starts a new job it can often feel a little overwhelming, so make sure they know you are there to help.

Strategy 5: Referral Relationships

Our natural inclination for self-preservation means that we often find ourselves asking, "What's in this for me?" There's nothing wrong with that question. However, if we are part of a business, we should also be asking, "What's in this for the business?"

Firms of accountants, lawyers, auditors, tax advisors and consultants are mostly full of highly motivated go-getters, ambitious for themselves and their careers. This results in high performance and business growth. However, there is a significant downside, in that this also leads to silo thinking and behaviour. Some trusted advisors become very territorial and possessive about their client relationships and are reluctant to bring others into meetings. Trusted advisors end up passing over business opportunities because there is limited benefit for them. In doing so, they fail to see the opportunities for their colleagues or the wider business.

The big four professional services firms have tried to address this challenge by advocating one firm behaviour, encouraging professionals to look out for opportunities for their colleagues. This requires a much broader level of understanding of the business as a whole. Most importantly, it is vital to encourage staff to build relationships across the business to the point where you trust your colleagues to introduce you to their clients and vice versa.

In recent years, a global firm closed all of their UK offices for an entire day and took every member of their team for a team-building event at the O2, one of the UK's largest concert venues. The event itself cost more than £1m and the loss of a day's work cost the firm around £10m. However, the financial benefit of increased morale and discretionary effort was worth infinitely more.

Maximising Growth

There is normally significant growth potential within the client portfolio that you already hold. In order to grow your business, there is no need to look far beyond the client relationships you already have. Maximising and expanding your existing relational ecosystem will always be the most efficient and effective way of growing your business. This approach requires a long-term view of the value of client relationships, a commitment to journey with them and to help them solve the real business issues that they face.

Key 3. Attract a Constant Stream of New Business

The dream way to grow your business is to grow a relational ecosystem that generates a constant stream of new business. You want the right sort of clients to be metaphorically 'knocking on your door', asking for your services. Well, the dream may not be as 'dreamy' as you first might think.

There are two main approaches to marketing. The first is 'interruption marketing', where you reach out to potential clients, often through paid advertising, to convince them that they need your services. This includes direct mail, email marketing, TV advertising, outbound call centres and trade shows.

The other approach is known as 'in-bound marketing', whereby you organically attract people into your relational ecosystem and clients into your business by earning, rather than buying, their attention. Earning rather than buying the attention of prospective clients does not mean it is free. Building the kind of reputation that attracts the right clients costs both time and money.

Personal Brand

Another word that is often used to describe our identity or reputation is personal brand. Whether we like it or not, we all have an identity, reputation and brand in the marketplace. It may be by design or by default. It may be well known or little known. It may be positive or it may be negative. It may attract clients or repel clients. Whatever the well-being and health of our personal brand, we all have one. The most powerful personal brands are those with the greatest degree of authenticity, congruence and alignment across the following four dimensions.

1. What are you known for?

One of the most powerful ways of understanding what you are known for is to know what it is that people say about you when you are not in the room. This can tell you all you need to know about your reputation and personal brand.

2. What do you want to be known for?

You should always have a clear idea of what you want to be known for and how you want to be seen. Without a clear vision of where you want to be, you can end up projecting a very vague and confusing image resulting in people being unsure what you stand for or what you actually do.

3. Who are you really?

Under the professionalism and confidence, there is also a real you waiting to get out. In today's marketplace, people are increasingly encouraged to bring their whole self to work to blend professional and personal lives because when people are most authentic, they are at their most engaged, most motivated and best performing.

4. What is your organisation known for?

What is your organisation known for and what does it want to be known for? If you and your organisation share the same values, reputation and aspirations, then you are heading for a potentially long and mutually beneficial relationship. If, however, you have a clash of values, you are heading for trouble. Your organisation is unlikely to change its values to accommodate you and you aren't any more likely to change your values either. So, if things are irreconcilable, it's time for one of you to make a move away from the other.

The more congruent these four dimensions are, the more powerful your personal brand will be; your relational ecosystem will be of a higher quality and the more prospective client relationships you will attract. Remember, it's not only about attracting clients, but about attracting the right quality of clients and retaining them.

Thought Leadership

For a service brand to attract business, it needs to position itself and its team as thought leaders who are constantly driving innovation and performance within its chosen sector. Thought leadership content can be packaged and placed on a myriad of in-bound marketing platforms, including social media, website search engine optimisation (SEO), Pay Per Click (PPC) advertising, lead magnets, blogging, vlogging, public speaking, book publishing and media.

In this Key, I want to get practical about three of the possible platforms – social media, public speaking and book publishing – which you can leverage to build your brand and relational ecosystem.

Platform 1: Social Media

One of the easiest ways to start positioning yourself as a thought leader is to engage in social media. There are always things to learn about connecting with your audiences and engaging them in something they love through social media. Here are my top seven tips:

Tip 1: Messaging
The rules of marketing apply to social media. The starting point is to know your audience – know their deepest needs and how you can address them before you start to craft your messaging. Part of knowing your audience is knowing what social media platform they use. You can add a call to action, but do so occasionally otherwise you'll annoy people and they'll stop following you. Your messaging should show that you are aware of current trends, issues or challenges within your field, and should help to showcase your own unique perspective.

Tip 2: Visuals
Pictures speak louder than words on social media, like in the rest of life, so wherever possible use a still picture or a very short video. Words and logos can be added to a still image to create memes. Very short films, of less than 60 seconds, always attract attention. You can do this with the inbuilt camera on your smartphone; simply hold the phone so you get a headshot view and then record a) introduction, b) main point and c) call to action. You can use a selfie stick if you haven't got a steady arm and a plug-in microphone if it's windy. Then you are ready to go.

Tip 3: Tags

Tags create another way for people to find what you post and increase your exposure. A location tag connects with people who are interested in that place. People tags drive you onto other people's social media feeds. Hashtags can connect you with other trending posts, including daily regulars such as #MondayMotivation #TuesdayThoughts #WednesdayWisdom #ThursdayThoughts #FridayFeelings #SaturdayMorning. Take a moment to review current tags that are relevant to your sector of work and keep on top of conversations taking place between your competitors, clients and potential clients.

Tip 4: Engagement

Social media is at its most powerful when it creates engagement. Each post creates an opportunity to have a conversation with your community rather than just to broadcast your message to the masses. If you engage with other people's posts, they are more likely to engage in yours. Remember, the majority of people don't engage on social media, so don't be discouraged by non-responsiveness. However, you might be surprised by the people who are passive followers simply watching you and absorbing the information that you are sharing.

Tip 5: Regularity

Consistency really matters in the world of social media. So, however often you decide to post, do it regularly. You can use software that enables you to preschedule posts – although I prefer to set an alarm to remind me to post at a particular time. This ensures that the content you post is relevant and picks up on any key trends taking place within your sector.

Tip 6: Email

Use your social media to build an email list by offering a free gift, otherwise known as a lead generator or lead magnet, when people subscribe to your newsletter. An email list has the advantage of enabling you to proactively contact people rather than passively waiting for them to respond to your posts. You can use apps like MailChimp. It's important to remember that General Data Protection Regulation 2018 is now in force across Europe, so you need to ensure that you comply with the regulations when you ask people to sign up to your email.

Tip 7: Pay Per Click (PPC)

Since internet search engines continually change their algorithms, it is increasingly hard to optimise websites and drive natural or organic traffic. Alongside updating the content on your website and ensuring that you use the language of your potential clients, you can also invest in Pay Per Click advertising so that platforms prioritise your post on a feed. You can set limits on the amount you spend and try setting different key words to see what is most effective.

Social media can help you cast your net broad and wide to reach and create lots of weak ties or bridging relationships that have the potential to connect you to ideas, opportunities and resources that you might not otherwise have access to.

Platform 2: Public Speaking

The American investor Warren Buffett once told a class of business students that he would pay anyone in the room $100,000 for 10 percent of their future earnings. If they were good communicators, he would raise his bid by 50 percent, because public speaking would make his 'investment' more valuable. Being a great public speaker attracts great relationships, which accelerates the growth of your relational ecosystem and consequently the growth of your business. So, here are my top seven public speaking tips:

Tip 1: Invitations through relationships
The secret of public speaking is that invitations don't arrive in the post, they arrive through relationships. So, if you want to start speaking in public or increase the number of opportunities you have for public speaking, invest in your relational ecosystem.

When you start describing yourself as a public speaker, people will ask you what you speak about. If it's of interest to them, they may invite you to speak at an event. The key to gaining more public speaking invitations and appointments is a combination of how you present yourself and building a powerful relational ecosystem amongst people who look for speakers at events.

Tip 2: Practice makes perfect
When you get started with public speaking, accept every invitation you receive in order to gain experience. As you become established, you can become more selective, choosing where you want to speak, who you want to speak to and what you want to speak about.

Professor Anders Ericsson at the University of Colorado wrote a paper, *The Role of Deliberate Practice in the Acquisition of Expert Performance* (1993). It highlighted the work of psychologists in Berlin, who had studied the deliberate practice habits of violin students. It discovered that the best violinists averaged more than 10,000 hours of practice, while the less-able performers had only completed 4,000 hours of practice. The psychologists didn't see any naturally gifted performers emerge and this surprised them. If natural talent had played a role, it wouldn't have been unreasonable to expect gifted performers to emerge after, say, 5,000 hours. Anders Ericsson concluded that, "Many characteristics once believed to reflect innate talent are actually the result of intense practice extended for a minimum of 10 years."

Malcolm Gladwell's book, *Outliers*, popularised this research and proposed 'the 10,000-hour rule', explaining that outstanding performance is the result of a significant amount of practice, not just innate talent. Whilst Gladwell's interpretation of Professor Ericsson's research has been questioned, the truth remains that practice makes perfect. A pilot's experience and expertise is measured by the number of 'flying hours'. In the same way, as a public speaker, practice makes perfect, so take every opportunity available to get in front of a crowd of whatever size and communicate yourself.

Tip 3: Call to action
It was a summer's afternoon on the terrace of the House of Commons, where I was gathered with a small group to hear about the work of a community charity. The occasion was buoyed by good company, a nice cup of tea and plentiful

clotted cream and jam scones. The Member of Parliament introduced the charity and then the CEO gave a thorough presentation about the charity's good work. At the end of the speech, thanks were given and we finished our conversations before heading home. Lovely as it was, I left asking why we had been there. There appeared little point to the gathering. If it was an attempt to raise money, then they clearly missed a trick as no one asked.

As Stephen Covey, author of *The 7 Habits of Highly Effective People,* wrote, 'Start with your end in mind.' Always begin preparing a talk by being absolutely clear about your purpose; know why and what call to action you are going to make. When you stand up to speak, remind yourself why you are there and what you are going to ask your audience to do as a result.

Tip 4: Know your audience well
There was a young public speaker who turned up to speak at an event. When he introduced himself, he asked if anyone in the room had heard him speak before. You can imagine his amazement when everyone raised their hands. The speaker then asked where they had met and they all said the previous week. At that moment, it dawned on him that the talk he was about to deliver was identical to the talk he had given to the same group just last week! Thankfully, he had another talk in his repertoire and so all went well, but it could have been a complete disaster.

Knowing your audience is essential, not just so that you don't repeat a talk or content that you have given before, but so that you meet the needs of the people who are listening to you. In preparing to deliver a keynote speech, I will ask the organiser to arrange for me to have a conversation with two or three people who will be in the audience. This is to help me understand the situation in which those I am speaking to are working in, so that I can be genuinely helpful to them. Every insight you can gain about your audience will help you empathise with them and speak into their life and work.

Tip 5: Create memorable content
The Vice President of Marketing for a global brand was delivering the keynote speech at a business conference I was attending. He was talking about the speed of product and market innovation and the need to change the development approach 'from plan and perfect to launch and learn'. This phrase has stuck with me ever since, so when I come across a team who is over-planning the development of a new product, I am reminded of the phrase 'from plan and perfect to launch and learn'.

Creating memorable content requires a lot of work. It is often about finding a counter-intuitive statement or a 'sticky phrase'. It means reading yourself full and writing yourself empty, playing around with words and phrases, and dipping into a dictionary and thesaurus until you create something memorable. Once you have found an anchor phrase, you can use it several times through your speech so that people remember it.

Tip 6: Have a natural conversation
My family and I were holidaying in the 'land of mouse' –

the Florida version. It was two weeks of Mickey and Minnie, southern fried food and American customer service, the latter of which is frankly unbeatable. One afternoon, we took a very popular ride, but the ride host spoke in a voice that sounded totally contrived and inauthentic. It actually distracted us from the whole experience of the ride.

The most powerful and authentic way of public speaking is to have a conversation with your audience. Whatever you do, don't develop a tone of voice that you use when you are public speaking. If you are relaxed as a speaker, then your audience will relax. If you speak effortlessly, your audience will listen effortlessly. If you speak authentically, then you will win your audience's trust.

Within that natural conversation, speak with passion, confidence and conviction, so that your audience are convinced by what you are saying. Whatever you do, don't be one of those speakers who have a soporific style that leaves the audience virtually comatose.

Tip 7: Master your stagecraft
I'm sure you've seen all sorts of painful examples of awkward speakers. Just as people speak in contrived and forced ways, they can also move around the stage with all the ease of a startled rabbit! Some speakers are so full of uncontrolled energy that they walk back and forth so much you feel like you are watching a game of tennis. You may have seen the industry guru who presents their years of experience using death by PowerPoint. Then, there is the presenter who timidly holds the microphone 12 inches from their mouth so

the amplification system is all but irrelevant. Perhaps you've also witnessed the speaker whose mannerism of playing with the loose change in their pocket totally distracts you from the message completely.

To master your stagecraft requires you to use your environment, resources and physicality to deliver the best possible speech or presentation to your audience. You might be public speaking on a large floodlit stage in front of thousands of people or you might be in a conference room with a dozen people.

Public speaking when done right is a powerful way of presenting 'brand you' and attracting new business opportunities.

Platform 3: Book Publishing

A book is the most powerful business card in the world because it transforms other people's perception of you. As a published author, you are perceived as an expert and world authority on the subject you have written about. So, publishing a book is a powerful way of building your brand, demonstrating that you are a thought leader and attracting the right sort of business. Writing a book may sound daunting if you have never done it before, but, trust me, it is easier that you think and here are my seven tips for making it happen:

Tip 1: Believe in yourself
Everyone has got a book in them and that includes you. I was in remedial english at school, I wasn't allowed to do computer

studies because my grasp of the english language wasn't good enough. I am highly dyslexic (I had to look up how to spell that!). I can read a book and retain absolutely nothing. I can talk for England, but I really struggle to write. I have now written more than ten books and write regularly for various publications including *The Times* newspaper. If I can write and publish a book, then so can you. Start by believing in yourself.

Tip 2: Write the back cover first

Decide on the subject you would like to write about. It does not need to be a subject that has never been written about before, because you will have your own unique perspectives and you also have your own unique audience who will want to read it. Start by writing the paragraph that will appear on the back cover of the book first. Some back cover paragraphs are blurb promoting the book and others a synopsis providing a summary. Pick up a few books and read the back cover paragraph and you will find examples that you could follow. Your back cover paragraph will become the compass that will help you keep on track as you write the book, so take time to wordsmith it.

Tip 3: What do I know now?

As Albert Einstein said, "The only source of knowledge is experience," so ask yourself the question, 'What do I know now (about your book's subject matter) that I wish I had known when I was starting out?' Begin to brainstorm thoughts and insights, writing them down as you go. Then, begin to play around with these points, crafting and sharpening them into chapter headings. Few people read long books nowadays, so think about how you might break 30,000 words into chapters. If you have lots to say and are a concise writer, you might want to think about more chapters of less words – for example, 30 chapters of 1,000 words each (two pages of typed A4). I've written a book with 101 secrets, which are 300–400 words each. Or you may have lots to say on a few subjects, so you could do 10 chapters of 3,000 words each. Play around with ideas and distill your brainstorm into the appropriate number of chapter headings.

Tip 4: Write a book like eating an elephant
Writing a book is like eating an elephant – the only way to do it is in bite-size chunks. Firstly, do NOT start writing, instead turn to the first chapter and think about the main things that you would like to say and record them as bullet points. Approach each chapter in turn and take the same approach. As you get going, feel free to hop backwards and forwards through the chapters noting bullet points and moving things around. If things come to mind that you want to say but you don't know where they will fit yet, no problem, simply start a page called 'Other Points' and make a note of them there. This will become a valuable source as the book emerges. As Lao Tzu said, "A journey of a thousand miles begins with a single step."

Tip 5: Adopt a writing lifestyle
A writing lifestyle that works for you depends on your personality. Some people like to carve out a month and go away and write, while others allocate time each week to sit down and write. Some set a daily word count target and others simply sit down and write until they are empty. Some people write best late at night and others early in the morning. For me, I wait for, or create, energy moments to write at my best. These are often in the morning and last for about three-hour

blasts and then I'm done and I need to go and do something else. The most important thing is that you find a habit and a discipline that works for you. As Jim Rohn said, "Motivation is what gets you started. Habit is what keeps you going."

Tip 6: Write first and edit second
The most important thing at this stage is to get the book out of you and onto a screen. It is tempting to stop and go back to read what you've written and start procrastinating about it. My advice is not to read through what you have written until you have finished the whole book. Once you have finished, go through the entire book from beginning to end and make improvements. At this stage, I will often leave the manuscript for a month and then go back to it afresh. My aim is only ever to get a manuscript 80 percent right, as trying to get the other 20 percent would kill me! As such, I engage the services of an editor who will work with my manuscript to take it to the next level. After that, I reread the manuscript to ensure none of the meanings have been lost and I engage a proofreader to go through the manuscript in detail. Teamwork is essential, especially when writing a book. As Mother Teresa said, "I can do things you can't do, you can do things I can't do, together we can do great things."

Tip 7: You don't need a publisher to get published
We have all heard horror stories about authors trying to find a publisher for their book, spending years sending their manuscript to different publishing houses and getting rejections or no reply at all. Publishing houses are businesses; your manuscript could be amazing or average, the thing they need to know is how many copies they could potentially sell.

If they back your book, they will try and place it in bookshops as well as online and perhaps audio version as well. Typically, traditional publishing will secure you an income of 15 percent of the cover price.

The alternative is to self-publish, which has the advantage of allowing you to control all the aspects of your book, including the title and cover design. However, you will be 100 percent responsible for the marketing of the book. By contrast, you will receive 85 percent of the cover price and 15 percent will cover the costs. Traditional publishers will try and persuade you that they can promote your book to a wider audience, which they can, but they'll be promising that to ten other books with the same publication month as yours and then move on to another ten the month after. I think you can probably tell what my preference is. As I've often said, if the door of opportunity isn't knocking, make a door!

Front of Mind

Social media, public speaking and publishing a book are powerful ways of building a brand and building a relational ecosystem that positions you as a thought leader. These are just three platforms you could use to attract new business, but there are many others you might wish to consider, such as writing blogs, articles and white papers. They all help you to remain at the forefront of your clients' minds and position you to attract the right kind of new business, while retaining the clients you already have.

Key 4. Leverage the Diversity Advantage

Diverse relationships have incredible impact on individuals, teams and organisations – creating greater performance and profitability.

The McKinsey research report, *Delivering through diversity* (2018), states that 'Gender-diverse companies are 21% more likely to outperform' and 'Racially-diverse companies are 33% more likely to outperform' their counterparts. They add that, 'While correlation does not equal causation, the correlation does indicate that when companies commit themselves to diverse leadership, they are more successful.'

It is my own experience of building businesses, NGOs and networks around the world that increasing the diversity of your relationships is extremely enriching personally and professionally.

Enhanced Capabilities

Diverse relationships and diverse teams, organisations and networks drive greater performance and profitability through five enhanced capabilities.

The first enhanced capability is the ability to access a diverse global talent pool. Recruiting from a diverse global talent pool enables a business to select from the greatest possible range of skills, expertise and knowledge. By doing so, the business is able to better compete on the global stage.

Greater engagement, discretionary effort and productivity is the second enhanced capability. In a diverse business, people are positively encouraged to bring their whole selves to work. In being a more authentic version of themselves, people are more engaged and motivated with colleagues, clients and in other stakeholder relationships.

Then, there is local market knowledge, insight and cultural sensitivity. When you have a diverse workforce, you benefit from having local relationships with customers and suppliers, speaking the local language and understanding cultural etiquette. All of these assets provide significant competitive advantage.

Fourthly, there is enhanced innovation, creativity and problem-solving. Different people see different perspectives, different possibilities and different panaceas. In seeing the world differently, people are able to create different, distinctive and differentiating solutions and added value. The alternative is a team or business where the majority of people are white, middle-class men who only ever come up with white, middle-class male ideas and solutions and leave much of the marketplace untapped.

The final enhanced capability is the ability to build a diverse relational ecosystem. Diverse and unlikely relationships create diverse and unlikely opportunities in life. If you feel you are stuck in your career or opportunities are not coming in the right quality or quantity, build a more diverse relational ecosystem and be open-minded to what you never expected.

These five enhanced capabilities are the areas where you and your business can create, sustain and leverage a competitive advantage in the marketplace.

'Snowy Peak Syndrome'

Despite the increased performance and profitability that these enhanced capabilities create, there remains a major lack of diversity within many sectors and companies.

This monochrome culture is particularly noticeable at executive levels of organisations. *The Guardian* newspaper recently described this as the 'snowy peak syndrome', explaining that, 'No matter how colourful the foothills and middle reaches of the average British organisation, the top is nearly always very white.' A research project conducted by Operation Black Vote and *The Guardian* showed that 'barely 3% of the most powerful, prominent 1,000 people in Britain are from ethnic minorities'.

These very same snowy peaks are also very male. The Deloitte 2015 report, *Women in the Boardroom*, explains that, 'The representation of women on corporate boards continues to increase, but the number of women leading boards still remains low globally. Overall, women now hold 12% of seats worldwide with only 4% chairing boards.' The World Economic Forum report, *Ten Years of the Global Gender Gap*, says that, 'Women face a gender wage gap globally, earning

77% of what men earn.' Gender inequality remains a challenge in the marketplace, especially at executive levels.

Race and gender are just two strands of many other protected characteristics of identity, such as age, sexuality and disability. Each of these strands contributes to the overall diversity of a business.

Prejudicial Bias

The shocking lack of business diversity in many societies is the result of all manner of discrimination, including racism and sexism. Discrimination on the basis of a person's identity has been, and remains, shockingly explicit within some societies. In other societies, discrimination continues to exist just as strongly within many of its institutions, whether business, politics or policing. Discrimination exists because of the prejudice that exists within many of our hearts and minds.

Inequality and prejudice are not the sole responsibility of people who are obviously racist and/or sexist. There are biases within all of us that lead us to make false assumptions about people. We all pre judge people (the meaning of prejudice) and treat them differently and wrongly as a result.

These biases have been formed by our upbringing, education, environment and experiences, and influence how we think about other people and therefore how we behave towards them. You may still be thinking 'no, not me', but as I describe seven biases I challenge you to not take ownership of at least one of them.

- 'Unconscious bias' is when our brains make quick judgements and assessments of people without us realising it. The brain tends to categorise people and things using easily identifiable criteria in order to save time and capacity. However, this means that we make assumptions that we are not even aware of.

- 'Affinity bias' occurs when we feel we have an affinity with a person. As a result of that affinity, we treat that person differently and act preferentially towards them in comparison to the way we treat those we do not have the same affinity with.

- 'Similarity bias' describes the natural human inclination to surround ourselves with people who are like us. As a result, we tend to be drawn to people we see parts of ourselves in and in the same way they are drawn to us because of the similarities.

- 'Attribution bias' explains that when we do something well, we tend to think it is due to our own merit and when something goes wrong, we think it is as a result of factors outside our control. When it comes to other people, we surprisingly tend to think the opposite. If someone else does something well, we tend to think they are simply lucky and when they do something badly, it is because of a fault in their personality or behaviour.

- 'Confirmation bias' explains that when we make an assessment of a person, we subconsciously look for evidence that backs up our pre-held beliefs about them.

So, if we believe that a person is slow, we will find examples of them being pedestrian or if we believe they are innovative, we will think of examples where they have displayed creativity. This happens because it is natural to want to be right. However, it is dangerous because our initial belief can be wrong.

- 'Beauty bias' influences us to think that the most attractive person will be most successful. For example, 60 percent of CEOs in the US are over six feet tall even though only 15 percent of the US population are of this height. This is just an illustration of the beauty bias in terms of how we think a CEO should look.

- 'Conformity bias', also known as 'group think' or 'peer pressure', is the tendency to behave similarly to those in a group, even if doing so goes against your own judgement. Most people want to be in the majority and so they will go along with the thinking, decisions and behaviour of the group to avoid being isolated, either alone or as part of a minority group.

Each of these biases causes us to make assumptions about other people and act in a prejudicial way towards them. Most people are not racist, sexist and ageist, but we all have biases that perpetuate societal and institutionalism discrimination.

Awareness and Intentionality

To strengthen diversity in our relational ecosystem and in our business, we firstly need to become aware of the discriminatory biases that each of us have and those that linger in the culture of the businesses we work for. Then, secondly, to make very clear, bold and strong choices in the people we hire, contract and do business with.

Life has programmed us all with biases that cause our inner processors to compute information in a prejudicial way. We can only change our biases when we become aware of what they are and how they are causing us to behave. To change a habit, you first need to be aware of it. We may have unconsciously held these biases for years and so reprogramming, and rewiring if necessary, takes some effort. The reprogramming is not a theoretical exercise; it happens by intentionally and deliberately making new decisions about relationships.

The NGO I lead is known as one of the most diverse. However, I recognise that there is still room for greater diversity. As a leadership team, we are deliberate about the people that are appointed to the boards and leadership teams. We do not hesitate to send back project proposals that do not have diverse teams involved. We practice positive discrimination in going out of our way to ensure that the voice of minority groups is heard and included.

Let's become intentionally inclusive in our relationships by not only choosing diversity when we have the choice but by proactively creating the opportunities to be more diverse.

Unlikely Opportunities

One of the greatest personal benefits to having a diverse relational ecosystem are the ideas, opportunities and resources it gives you access to.

Professor Mark Granovetter of Stanford University observed that the strong ties we build tend to be homogenous relationships with people who are like us, because 'like attracts like'. By contrast, the weak ties we create tend to be heterogenous relationships with people unlike us, because we struggle with difference.

Strong ties are really important to us; they are with people who we know well and can depend on. These are also known as 'bonding relationships'. Weak ties are important because they are with people unlike us and therefore provide us access to different ideas, opportunities and resources. As a result, they are also known as 'bridging relationships' and provide us with genuine advantage. It is these bridging relationships that help us build a diverse relational ecosystem and in time these bridging relationships can become 'bonding relationships'.

In business diversity is a powerful source of competitive advantage so lets grasp it.

Key 5. Get Over Yourself. You Are in the Way

A social anxiety survey of over 3,000 adults found that people's number one fear was speaking in front of a group. A *New York Times* article, *Social Anxiety* (1984), explained, 'Shyness, the most common form of social anxiety, occurs when a person's apprehensions are so great that they inhibit his making an expected or desired social response. Symptoms of shyness can be as minor as avoiding eye contact when speaking to someone, or as major as avoiding conversations whenever possible.'

The greatest obstacle to people proactively building a relational ecosystem of client relationships is confidence. You may think that relational confidence is the last thing highly educated, qualified and accomplished professionals lack, but you would be surprised. Sometimes, it is those people who outwardly seem most together who are wrestling their greatest fears inside.

A lack of relational confidence can also cause professionals to send an email rather than pick up the telephone, even though they know a telephone call will produce a significantly better response. A confidence deficit can cause people to passively wait to be introduced rather than gently asking for an introduction, recommendation or referral. It can also result in professionals having an over-reliance on the notes in their day book and the presentation on their deck of slides, rather than on their personal qualities.

The most powerful confidence doesn't derive from what we know, what we've done or what status we have. Confidence is about being comfortable with our own identity, being comfortable around other people and being comfortable in our interactions with those individuals, even those who are very different from us. This may sound obvious, but time and time again a lack of relational confidence is the main obstacle that causes professionals to hang back in client relationships and building the relational ecosystem they need.

There are four possible quadrants out of which our behaviour derives:

Quadrant 1: Arrogance

Many large companies undertake brand surveys with their clients to provide feedback on how they are performing. The results of these brand surveys among the big four professional service firms tell us that clients can perceive them as being arrogant. This has to be understood in the context that firms are hired by clients because of their expert knowledge and insights. However, this doesn't excuse the perception of arrogance. This arrogance is most often unintended; it derives from insecurity rather than security. It's a natural response that smart people who feel insecure often hide behind their knowledge, but it doesn't endear them to clients.

Arrogance is fundamentally about having an attitude that we are more important than other people or that other people are not as important as we are. These arrogant attitudes cause people to behave in superior ways towards others and result in poor business relationships. By contrast, if we show respect to others, they will reciprocate and show respect to us.

Quadrant 2: Inferiority

If you are with a client who is particularly powerful, wealthy or beautiful, it can create feelings of intimidation and insecurity. It is all too easy to compare ourselves with other people and see all the ways in which they are superficially superior to us.

Over the years, I have come to realise that particularly powerful, wealthy and beautiful people are not different to you and me; they have their own worries and concerns. Powerful people are concerned about who is going to stab them in the back; wealthy people worry about whether they have got enough money; and beautiful people worry about getting old and losing their looks.

Most people are not arrogant, they do not think of themselves more highly than they should. In fact, they think the opposite. Most people I meet do not think of themselves as highly as they should. This negative self-belief becomes disabling and disempowering when building relationships with other people.

Quadrant 3: Timidity

Some people live in a place of timidity. They don't think about themselves or others as highly as they really should. They tend to hibernate. Although they may be in the room, office or meeting, they will be withdrawn and you could be forgiven for not noticing they are present. They often miss out on the opportunity to make their contribution and others miss out on the chance to hear their unique perspective. It's also likely that timid people won't build strong relationships with either colleagues or clients.

As a result, they fail to reach their professional potential or, for that matter, potential in the other areas of their life.

Quadrant 4: Confidence

As professionals, the place we operate from – or, should I say, aim to operate from – is the place of confidence. The confident professional has a positive and realistic perspective of themselves and of others.

Relational confidence is more complex than it first appears. Confidence can be found in many places, and many people find confidence in what they know. When it comes to client relationships, this kind of confidence is good as long as the client stays on track with what we know and within our comfort zone. The challenge is when a client chooses to go off-piste.

There is a contrast and even a tension between knowledge-based confidence and identity-based confidence. Within the world of professional services, there are lots of very smart people who are hired to provide their knowledge and insight to clients. The challenge is that their confidence is often found in what they know rather than who they are. It is all too easy to hide behind intellect.

The challenge we face is to move from knowledge-based confidence to identity-based confidence. In my experience, there are two routes. The first route is through invited learning interventions, such as increased self-awareness, appraisals, feedback, coaching, mentoring, training and peer-learning groups. These interventions are good, but they can take time to sink in. The second route to developing identity-based confidence is through uninvited learning experiences, which are the painful things in life like failure, relational breakdown or ill health. As long as you are willing to reflect upon these and use them as learning opportunities, then as the philosopher Freiderick Nietzsche wrote, 'what doesn't kill you will make you stronger'.

Bad Moments

It's one thing leading a project, team or organisation, but leading ourselves is another competence all together. A key part of self-leadership is understanding where our behaviour might regress and what to do about it.

The reality is that whilst we aim to live and lead from a place of confidence, we all have bad moments and bad days. These dips can cause us to retreat to a place of arrogance, inferiority or timidity. In my experience, there are three triggers that can cause this behaviour. Providing we can identify the triggers, we can control our response.

Trigger 1: Gremlins

To say that I did not do well at school is somewhat of an understatement. I was in remedial maths and remedial english and left school with my confidence in tatters. As a result, I grew up with the belief that I was stupid. This gremlin ravaged me for years. Whenever something went wrong, I said it was because I was stupid. When I didn't win the opportunity or the contact, I would quietly say to myself that it was because I was stupid.

Even after I completed a Bachelors Degree and two Masters Degrees, I still heard the voice inside my head telling me I was stupid. When I published my first book or won my first blue chip contract, I believed it was a fluke. It has taken me a couple of decades to overcome this 'gremlin' and to live and lead from a place of confidence.

If we are honest, we all have gremlins that play negative messages in our heads. On good days, we may not hear them at all, but when things start to get difficult or start to go wrong, the gremlin voice seems to play its destructive message over and over again.

It takes a lot of focus, effort and determination to turn down the volume of our gremlins and lean into our inner confidence so we can achieve all that we are capable of.

Trigger 2: Stress

On other occasions, the pressures we are living with cause us to have bad moments or a bad day. To a point, pressure helps us to perform; it creates positive energy that produces the adrenalin we need to rise to a challenge, but there is a level at which pressure can turn into stress and we feel like everything is getting on top of us.

There are plenty of stressful things that can happen at home, like moving house, tension in our marriage, problems with our children, ill health, disagreements with neighbours or financial challenges. We are not machines and none of us can switch off from personal matters in a professional context. When personal matters are difficult, the best we can try to do is minimise the impact on our professional work.

At work, there are stressful times when the deadlines come thick and fast, when we make a mistake, when we are criticised by other people, when team relationships are difficult or when we fail to win a new contract. We feel as though we are struggling to keep our head above water and so again our confidence is knocked and we spiral into ineffectiveness.

To make it through these times of stress, we sometimes need to simply keep on keeping on until we make it to the end. It might be confiding in a friend or a colleague and asking for their help, or stepping away from the situation to get some fresh perspective in order to regain our confidence so we can tackle what's in front of us.

Trigger 3: Power Dynamics

It's not always an internal issue – such as a gremlin or stress –
that triggers a loss in confidence. Often pressure is produced
by external events that we are coping with at work. There are
power dynamics at work that can intimidate, exclude and be
prejudiced against us. These dynamics often centre around
age, race and gender. Too often, the powerful or majority
voice is heard whilst the least powerful or minority voices are
silenced or ignored.

One example is the significant prejudices in business felt by
women and ethnic minority groups. The number of women
on FTSE companies has increased from 12.5 percent in
2010 to 26 percent in 2016 and the 2016 Lord Davies British
government report, *Women on Boards*, has set a target of 33
percent by 2020. At the same time, *A Report into the Ethnic
Diversity of UK Boards*, conducted by Sir John Parker, found
that only 8 percent of all FTSE directors were non-white.
There are clearly power dynamics at work that prejudice
against certain groups, which we need to overcome.

Power dynamics vary from culture to culture. In some contexts,
being young is venerated and increases influence; in others,
being old is more highly respected because it is synonymous
with wisdom and commands respect. Sometimes, being
black makes you an ethnic minority whose voice isn't heard
adequately, while in other contexts being white makes you an
ethnic minority. Some cultures are fully awakened to gender
equalities and there are some in which the power imbalance
remains.

So, how can we overcome power dynamics? When we are in the majority, it's important to recognise the power that comes with it, so we can invite minority voices to be heard. When we are in the minority, it's important to recognise that we have to consciously be assertive to ensure that we are heard.

Professionally Confident

As we strive to increase our effectiveness, it's important to remember we are all human with natural default levels of relational confidence. We all have our good days and our bad days. By recognising our gremlins, times of stress and the balance of power dynamics, we can work to overcome them and find a place of professional confidence. It's only then, in this place of confidence, that we can be the best possible version of ourselves and build the relational ecosystem we need.

Maintain Your Relational Ecosystem

The second priority in building a relational ecosystem is to maintain the relationships that you initiate. Some people find going out and meeting new people a very comfortable thing to do, whilst others find it a real challenge. Regardless of how you feel about creating new relationships, there is no point in doing so if you are going to do no more than send your new contact an email afterwards to say it was nice to meet.

Despite the incredible difference that relationships make in our lives, most people are passive about maintaining relationships. It is my experience that no more than 5 percent of people are proactive about maintaining the relationships in their ecosystem and more than 95 percent of people are passive.

One of the best illustrations of proactivity and passivity is the use of business cards. People may ask for your business card, or you may offer it, but more than 95 percent of people that take your card will never contact you again. The vast majority of people only react when someone directly contacts them. There is a rare breed of no more than 5 percent of the population who are intentional and deliberate about sustaining and developing the relationships they start.

We can distinguish ourselves within our business, sector and the marketplace by deciding to be on the front foot about building relationships and joining the 5 percent of the population who are intentional, deliberate and proactive. The question you need to ask yourself is, 'Am I naturally proactive or passive about building relationships?' If you fall into the passive category, how are you going to become more proactive?

The second section of this book explores four keys that will enable you to become world-class in maintaining your relational ecosystem.

Key 6. Sell Without Selling

I will never forget the morning I spent with a professional services business talking about their direct entry on-boarding process. Each year, as a firm, they promoted a number of internal candidates, as well as a number of external candidates into the firm at partner level. The external candidates brought to the firm new capability, essential experience and marketplace contacts. The candidates were offered a 'golden handshake' in excess of six figures, plus a very attractive partner package. I was meeting with the firm on this occasion to discuss a number of failed on-boarding situations where the integration of new team members had gone wrong. On face value, everything looked great for these direct entry partners; everyone was so friendly and the on-boarding journey was thorough and rigorous.

After twelve months, a number of these partners had problems with stress, health or simply wanted out. What was going wrong? The answer could be found in the firm's relational ecosystem. What the direct entry partners or the firm didn't realise was exactly how individualistic, territorial and protective other partners were in their parts of the business. Whilst individuals were initially very friendly, attitudes soon changed. The business had world-class systems and processes and yet, as always, the fastest, simplest and easiest way to get anything done is through trusting relationships. These direct entry partners hadn't grown up inside the firm and therefore hadn't naturally got to know people across the lines of service and functions, so they found it really difficult to get things done as they simply didn't know who to ask.

I tell this story because the way you integrate new people into established systems can be a huge challenge. How do you take someone you have just met and integrate them into your relational ecosystem where there are established relationships that have been cultivated over many years? Maintaining a client relationship you have had for years alongside a new relationship with a prospective client requires some intentional effort on your part.

Qualifying

Being an authentic relationship builder means you have to be open to connecting with anyone. However, you can't simply go around investing in relationships with lots of people hoping one of them might become a client. Business sustainability and growth requires you to qualify relationships by ascertaining whether they are a prospective client you need to get to know or whether they are an interesting person who it is nice to keep in contact with from time to time.

This qualifying process isn't about whether you are going to bother to connect and on-board a person into your ecosystem or not, it's about what level of time, energy and resources you are going to invest into building a relationship with them. Authenticity means we treat everyone well simply because it's the right thing to do. There is also a powerful business case for this based on three principles: first, you don't always know who a person is; secondly, you don't know who they might know; and thirdly, you don't know who they might become. So, even if you are not going to invest heavily in the relationship at this stage, it is still very important that you on-board the relationship into your relational ecosystem.

In this Key, I will examine the seven steps to effectively on-boarding a person into your relational ecosystem.

Step 1: Business Cards

When you meet that person that you connect with there is the inevitable exchange of business cards. One challenge I often find is that the people I'm interested in keeping in contact with haven't got a business card – they might have left it in another suit or handbag, or they might have simply run out.

My advice is to never rely on giving out your business card in the hope that someone will send you their details. If you give someone a business card, it is highly likely that you will never hear from them again. As the 95/5 principle explains: 95 percent of people are reactive and 5 percent of people are proactive. 95 percent of people do nothing with the business cards they are given and no more than 5 percent will bother to follow through.

So, I always carry a pen and a pocket jotter – a small leather board with four corners, under which can be tucked appropriately sized pieces of paper – in my suit pocket for just such occasions. So, when someone says, "Sorry, I haven't got a business card, but if you give me yours I'll email you my details," I reply, "Oh, don't worry about that, just jot your email and mobile on here." It works every time.

Step 2: Follow Through or Fail

Now, be honest, how many times have you emptied out your suit pocket when you take it to the dry cleaners only to discover a business card you were given at an event months ago? We all do it, but if we fail to connect with the people we meet, then we will fail in business full stop. If we do not follow up contacts we make at an event, then we might as well have not bothered going in the first place. My experience is that the vast majority of people do not follow through with the people they meet.

I recently delivered a Relationology Masterclass about achieving business growth through relationships. The client was a private bank and during the programme, I explained to one of the participants that I would be interested in opening a bank account. It's hard to believe, but I waited months for a reply. There I was, a prospect who fitted their client profile, with cash to deposit in their bank. When I finally received a reply, I had already decided I would not work with someone who operated on those kind of time scales.

Personally, I aim to follow through with people within forty eight hours of meeting them face-to-face. You can immediately differentiate yourself in your business and the wider marketplace by promptly following through with the people you meet.

Step 3: Social Media Connection

Over the years, I have developed the habit of sitting down once a week and reviewing who I have met, and connecting with them on their preferred social media platform. Now and again I meet someone who doesn't 'do' social media, but they are becoming an increasingly rare and extinct species.

For business people, my first port of call is LinkedIn, because it is viewed as the preferred business social media platform. If people are working in NGOs, I tend to find them on Facebook; if they are younger professionals, I find them on Instagram.

Social media is a powerful way of creating a connection between people, so that you can find each other again if you want to. The other main benefit is that if you pop up on other people's social media feeds, it helps you remain at the forefront of their mind. You can increase the frequency you pop up on people's social media feeds by investing a little money in PPC (Pay Per Click), which means the social media platform or publisher increases your prominence because you pay them each time someone clicks on the link in your social media post.

Step 4: Email Opt-In

Once I have followed through with someone and established an initial connection, I will often ask if they would like to receive my weekly video blog, *A Minute with Matt*. Each week, I publish a 60 second video blog in which I talk about someone

I've met that week and something I've learnt from them about relationships. As someone who works internationally, I try and find an interesting backdrop to film, be it a canal in Amsterdam, outside the Kremlin in Moscow or on safari in Africa. *A Minute with Matt* is then published online and I email it to the community of people who have signed up to receive it. I use this opportunity to help my community in business relationships and to remain at the front of their minds.

Of course, it's important that you follow best practice and respect the preferences of clients and potential clients when you contact them. Legislation in the form of the European General Data Protection Regulation 2018 means that people need to actively opt-in in order to be added to your email list and you need to have public privacy policy defining your use of people's data.

One of the ways you can inspire people, particularly those you haven't met, to sign up to an email list is to offer them an initial free gift. In the trade, this is referred to as a 'lead generator' or 'lead magnet' because it provides the name and email of someone who is interested in what you have written about. Currently, the Relationology 'lead generator' is a free copy of my popular eBook 7 *Behaviours of Highly Effective Relationship Builders*.

Step 5: Ad hoc Contact

You will naturally be reminded of the people within your relational ecosystem from time to time. They might pop up on your social media feed, be mentioned by someone else or their name might pop out as you flick through your digital 'little black book'. Alternatively, you might come across an interesting article, blog, video or book that reminds you of them. These occasions are the perfect opportunity to make contact with them. You don't need a business reason – in fact, it's always best to build a relationship with someone before you need anything from them – so use the opportunity to reach out.

Look for ad hoc opportunities, reasons or excuses to get in touch with people in your relational ecosystem. Relationships are a contact sport; you need to touch them to keep them alive and to save them from drifting away.

Since all our inboxes are crammed, I prefer to contact people in ways other than email. When I first meet someone, I try to ensure I obtain their mobile telephone number as these ad hoc points of contact are quite natural to do by text message or other SMS platform.

Step 6: Face-to-face Meeting

You are now in a position where you have created a number of connection points between you and another person. If, on further examination, the person qualifies as a prospective client, then a face-to-face meeting is often the most natural next step. I know this sounds obvious, but sometimes even the most experienced professionals can hesitate at this point. The greatest distance in the world is between knowing what to do and doing it.

This step might actually happen as part of 'Step 2: Follow Through or Fail', because it is clear from day one that the person you have met is someone you could help. Alternatively, it might be something you work towards or consider over time. You might meet somebody face-to-face and, even though there are no immediate opportunities, you might agree to meet again in three months, six months or even in a years time. You might put a prompt in your diary for when it might be good to meet with the person face-to-face again.

The purpose of such meetings is to build a genuine relationship focused on understanding that person's deepest felt needs and those of their team and organisation.

Step 7: Proposal or Referral

When you are exploring whether you can help a client with their deepest felt need, it is really important that you do not immediately see yourself as a solution to their problem. First, you need to view yourself as a problem-solver who can support them in identifying the solution. Some people believe their product or service is the solution to everybody's problem and they never genuinely stop to truly understand the issue that needs solving and indeed who the best person to address that need really is. Only when you truly understand the deepest felt needs of your client do you know with confidence and conviction whether you can help them. If that is the case, then, like a sniper, surgeon or striker, you can offer assistance with precision and accuracy.

Once a prospect has identified a specific business need, I encourage them to quantify it in numbers. To think about what the opportunity cost of doing nothing and also about the financial upside for the business if they could address the challenge. These numbers become critically important in motivating the prospect to invest in doing something about the business need.

If your prospect reaches the point where they believe you can help them solve their business challenge, you will agree to prepare a proposal. I have learnt that simply sending them such a proposal can leave you waiting. So, instead, I agree with them when to send a proposal and when exactly to have a follow-through conversation to discuss how it meets their expectations. In this way, I am able to positively move towards the contracting and delivery stage.

If you are not the solution to your client's problem, then the best thing you can do for yourself and for your client is to refer them to someone else who can help. This may be an internal referral within your business or an external referral to another trusted provider. Don't see this as a loss of business, but as the development of trust between you and your client. Who knows what may come as a result of the support you have provided.

The 'No-Sell Sell'

As you know well by now, I hate networking and I hate selling. The relational ecosystem on-boarding journey that I've outlined above can be described as a 'no-sell sell'. It is my experience that people hate to be sold to, but they do love to buy. What I mean by this is that people hate salespeople turning up and trying to sell their product or service to anything that moves, regardless of need. Instead, your focus should be on building a genuine relationship and getting to know each other. If you are the answer to what each other is looking for, it will quickly become apparent. This is the 'no-sell sell'.

Key 7. Keep in Contact With Everyone You Know

One of the most frequent questions I am asked is, 'How do you keep in contact with everyone you know?' As we develop our relational ecosystem, the number of prospects, clients, intermediaries, advocates, colleagues and suppliers we are expected to keep in contact with can become overwhelming.

Recently, I was asked by the *Harvard Business Review* (HBR) to write an article about this subject in response to a number of HBR readers who felt overwhelmed by the number of relationships they were trying to maintain. As life goes on, you naturally acquire more relationships and as you move through roles and become more successful, you collect people on the way. Before you know it, you feel swamped by all the people you know.

In the article, I explained, 'The feeling of being overwhelmed can paralyse us — like a rabbit caught in the headlights of an oncoming car, we freeze, not knowing which way to go. Or we can try to please everyone by saying yes to everything — like a rabbit hopping randomly all over a garden. By attempting to do everything, we exhaust ourselves. And whichever way we react, we never get where we want to go. There is an alternative to people paralysis and people pleasing: review your relational ecosystem and recalibrate your relationship priorities so that you can allocate your resources accordingly.'

The reality is simple; you can't have the same relationship with everyone you know. In this Key, I will show how you can filter and prioritise your relationships in a way that retains your integrity and authenticity, and at the same time enables you to remain sane.

Differentiation Relationships

Differentiating your relationships can make your relational ecosystem of clients, prospects, introducers, refers and intermediaries maintainable and sustainable.

For most businesses, the process of differentiating relationships is done very discretely. However, some businesses are very transparent about the way they manage relationships to build customer loyalty.

British Airways differentiates customers very openly. It has an Executive Club, which is a loyalty programme that incentivises customers to fly with them rather than other airlines. The Executive Club has bronze, silver and gold tiers, which provide access to more and more benefits, including advance seat selection, additional luggage allowances, fast-track security, access to executive lounges, priority boarding and extra air mile allowances. Customers work up the tiers depending upon how often, how far and how well they travel – in other words, how much cash they spend with the company. This is a powerful example of differentiating customer relationships according to their importance to a business.

Not-for-profit organisations also differentiate their donor relationships given that the majority of their income will derive from a minority of their supporters. The not-for-profit will value all their donors and have a regular communication programme. However, their major donors will have a contact programme that is far more personalised, providing access to the Chief Executive and other key leaders. Without these major donors, the not-for-profits would become unsustainable and so it is critical to invest in those relationships more deeply.

The same approach of differentiating relationships can be applied to your relational ecosystem. A minority of relationships in your ecosystem will be responsible for producing the majority of your business revenue, so it makes sense to deploy the majority of your time, energy and resources with them. In this way, you can prioritise your most important relationships but always have something to give to the other people you know. The 'networker' approach would be to focus all your resources on top relationships and discard those that can't help.

Regardless of whether you run an airline, charity or a personal relational ecosystem, you can differentiate your relationships with authenticity.

Pareto Principle

So, how do you begin to differentiate the relationships in your ecosystem, whether those in your portfolio, pipeline or wider population?

In the *Harvard Business Review* article I mentioned earlier, I suggested using the Pareto 80/20 principle in order to differentiate relationships in your relational ecosystem. In this way, you can deploy the majority (80 percent) of your time, energy and resources with the minority (20 percent) of your relationships. You can then keep back a minority (20 percent) of your time, energy and resources for the majority (80 percent) of your relationships. In this way, you can maintain authenticity and avoid becoming a networker who dumps people who aren't immediately useful.

The Pareto Principle can also be applied to a prospective client pipeline of any trusted advisor. Again, exceptions can be found, but typically 20 percent of prospects represent 80 percent of top-line growth and the other 80 percent of clients just 20 percent of revenue growth. Being able to differentiate clients in this way then informs marketing spend and investment in relationship management. With your top 20 percent of relationships, you invest primary time with bespoke communications and one-to-one personal meetings. With the other 80 percent of your relationships, you rely on more generic communications and events. In this way, you are able to treat everyone well and sustain your relational ecosystem and sanity.

I was recently working with a private banking client who had a unique challenge. They were providing a top level of service to all their clients, but couldn't grow their business unless they began to differentiate their portfolio. As part of the solution to this challenge, they were investing in a 'high-tech and high-touch strategy', in which a new app would enable clients with less complex needs to complete their financial transactions via a smartphone, but maintaining personal telephone support for more complex financial needs.

Long Lists and Short Lists

I'm not sure if I'm the sort of person who loves lists or simply that my world would fall apart if I did not write them.

When it comes to business development, I keep it simple. I have two lists: my short list is for business development opportunities that need seizing now and my long list is for business development opportunities that I will pursue later. My short list includes following through on an asset management client who asked if they could book me to speak at some more events – this is definitely an opportunity that needs grasping now. Another example is responding to the CEO of a private bank who I already work with and wants to introduce me to a 'C suite' executive of another major financial institution, who could become a new client in my portfolio – this is also a short list opportunity.

By comparison, my long list of business development opportunities are things I can follow up on later. For example, about a decade ago, I picked up the name of a partner in a big four professional services firm who sounded like the sort of person I would like to be connected to. There was no immediate reason or access point to meet with him, so I added his name to my long list and waited for an opportunity to emerge.

He remained on my long list for seven years, in which time he had become a senior partner in the firm and so the stakes had been raised and, in many senses, the chances of me finding a potential opportunity to meet him had significantly reduced. I then had the opportunity to take a guest to a private luncheon for twenty people with the leader of a political party who shortly afterwards became the Prime Minister. So, I wrote to the gentleman and invited him to be my guest. He replied immediately to say that he'd be delighted and asked me to visit his office on the day in question so his chauffeur could take us to the lunch. Various conversations and meetings followed, during which time my business was invited to become an approved supplier of the big four professional services firm, which has made doing business with them a lot easier ever since.

Another long list opportunity example is an executive who announced that he was moving on from his current employer to a new business I had not done work for. His name went on my long list for six months so he could complete his gardening leave and get his feet under the table at his new firm. The six months has now passed and I've just arranged lunch so we can explore possibilities of working together again.

Running a business development short list and long list means I always know what my immediate priorities are and I'm always building a bigger pond of possibilities I can choose to draw from at any time.

Prioritisation

Once you have differentiated relationships in your relational ecosystem, the challenge is about prioritisation and effective time management. There are many different ways to increase productivity and performance and my top ten tips are as follows:

Undertake your most important work when you are at your most energised. It is easy to put off the work you find the hardest until later or another time. The problem is that you are then least able to complete it because you are less energised and at your most fatigued.

Always ask 'why?'. Start with the end in mind. Know why you are doing something and what the outcome will be before you start. Use the 'Triple A' strategy: A for Appointment; when you consider an appointment in the diary, stop and ask questions. A for Aim; why am I doing this? A for Action; what action could I take as a result?

Delegate responsibility to a personal assistant or to other members of your team. There is a big difference between delegating tasks that result in micro-management and delegating responsibility where people can see things through from beginning to end.

Utilise smartphone apps to save time, effort and money. You can scan expense receipts and throw the paper version away, book and check-in for flights, raise quotations and invoices, order thank you flowers – the list goes on and on.

Pre-qualify meetings by asking people why they want to meet. It may be that you could both achieve what you would like with a 10-minute telephone conversation rather than a 60 minute meeting. Alternatively, having talked on the telephone, it may be more appropriate for them to meet someone else.

Rise early so you can get important work done before you will be disturbed. Different sectors have different start times so you can call some people at 7 am and others will only be available after 9 am.

Create defined windows in your day when you go online to email or engage in social media. For example, I set my alarm for 5 pm each day (it's when my community in the United States is also awake) to post and respond on my social media.

Cluster similar tasks together by adding them to a simple list that you come back to later and then complete all at once. It takes a lot less time to do five similar tasks at the same time rather than separately.

Refer opportunities to people you are coaching, mentoring and managing, so as to provide them with opportunities they might not otherwise have had. This is a great way to raise a team who can support you – and you never know where these individuals might end up in the future!

At the start of every day and every week, write a to-do list so you know what you want to achieve before your start.

'Friends'

I try not to use the 'F' word in business, but please excuse me just this once. You can't be friends with everybody, but you can be friendly with everybody. To maintain levels of service excellence, grow your business and protect your own health and well-being, it's essential to differentiate relationships. This can only be achieved by filtering your relationships with integrity and prioritising some relationships over others.

Key 8. Increase Your Impact Overnight

We all know people who have a powerful personal impact due to their compelling charisma. Most of us, however, don't believe we have the charismatic charm that naturally inspires the devotion of others. But all is not lost; we should be encouraged by Richard Wiseman, Professor of Public Understanding of Psychology at the University of Hertfordshire, who suggested in his study on *Charisma* (Famelab 2005) that 50 percent of charisma is innate, but 50 percent is learned behaviour. So those of us without bucketloads of natural charisma can develop the learned behaviours that will increase our personal impact on our relational ecosystem.

Executive Presence

A recent survey by the Center for Talent Excellence explained that 'executive presence' counts for 26 percent of what it takes to get promoted. Two-thirds of people surveyed described that 'executive presence' as the ability to project gravitas, confidence, poise under pressure and decisiveness. Nearly 60 percent said that sounding uneducated negatively affects executive presence and three-quarters said that unkempt attire distracts from your executive presence. Overall, the survey highlighted the importance not only of what you say, but of the way you present yourself as a whole person.

This idea that words are only one way to make an impact is also put forward by the African American poet, biographer and civil rights activist, Maya Angelou, who said that, "People will forget what you said, people will forget what you did, but people will never forget how you made them feel." Actions speak louder than words and people really aren't interested in what we know until they know how much we care about them.

In this Key, I will look at the five dimensions that can help you to increase your charisma, executive presence and likeability through, what I call, 'personal impact'.

Dimension 1: At Ease or On Edge

I remember arriving at a large venue to speak at a special event and being escorted into the green room. There were a number of other guests being looked after by the hospitality team. I'm not sure how to describe it other than to say there was an uncomfortable silence, so I broke the ice and walked around the room introducing myself to people and starting conversations. Silence between people who know each other well can be completely comfortable, but silence between strangers or vague acquaintances can be very awkward.

Some hotels have a wonderful way of making you feel completely at home the moment you arrive, whilst in others the staff behave like you are an inconvenience. There is an international hotel group, in which I have been hosted by clients, who have a team of 'ladies in red' that meet you at the door of the hotel and ensure you are at ease from the moment you arrive until the moment you leave. Similarly, there is a quintessentially English hotel in London whose maître d' is the most wonderful host; he always welcomes you, finds the best place for you to sit and takes care of you throughout your time at the hotel.

The first dimension of personal impact is whether you make clients feel at ease or on edge. As a trusted advisor, there are some business meetings you walk into where you feel on edge from the moment you step into the room, because there is no small talk and the atmosphere feels starchy. Alternatively, when you feel at ease with people, you will be inclined to want to work with them.

Dimension 2: Special or Insignificant

I know two senior executives who are friends, but are also absolute polar opposites in the way they make other people feel. The first is a senior business executive who talks about himself quite a lot. He talks about the incredible places he goes, the incredible people he meets and what they said to him. After spending time with this gentleman, you get the feeling that you are of little significance to him at all and generally feel about a foot tall. The other gentleman is always more interested in the person he is meeting. He will ask you where you have been, who you have met and what they have said to you. Somehow, he very naturally gets you talking about yourself, your hopes, fears and dreams. You leave any encounter with him buoyed with self-confidence and feeling about a foot taller than you really are. The totally different impact that two people can have on you and their contrasting levels of likability is incredible.

The second dimension of personal impact is about whether you make people feel special or insignificant. You will naturally want to be around people who make you feel the most authentic and special version of yourself. You will want to avoid those who make you feel small and insignificant. As trusted advisors, let's ensure that we leave our clients feeling the right way!

Dimension 3: Appreciated or Taken for Granted

There are people who are more likely to appreciate others and there are people who are more likely to take others for granted. It is easier to appreciate those people who do the extraordinary, remarkable and special things because we notice them more. Those that are there day in and day out, are totally reliable and just get on with things without a fuss, however it is too easy to take them for granted. It's easy to overlook these people within a team, client relationship, family or friendship group.

If a person is taken for granted long enough, it can lead to resentfulness and a withdrawal from the relationship. There is an old saying that goes, 'Familiarity breeds contempt.' It is all too easy to become too familiar in our relationships, whether with a friend, a colleague or a client, which can lead to us taking them for granted. The converse is also true; if a person feels appreciated, they will lean into the relationship, which creates an opportunity for greater connection and commitment.

The third dimension of personal impact is about whether we make people feel appreciated or taken for granted.

Some clients will do extraordinary things, whilst others will be stable, consistent and reliable, and it's important we appreciate both.

Dimension 4: Giver or Taker

Business people can be broadly grouped into two categories: givers and takers. Givers are generous; their natural disposition is to contribute to the lives of the people around them. They enter every meeting and encounter with a focus on helping the person they are meeting to achieve what they desire. They do this without expecting anything in return and develop a reputation as someone who is committed to other people's success as well as their own.

Takers, by contrast, are consumers who will take everything you ever give them and still look for more. Takers are stingy; their default position is to be happy to receive from others, but they are unlikely to be generous themselves. They easily take advantage of givers. People who persistently take from others whilst rarely or never giving will lose respect and they will damage their reputation.

Adam Grant, in his book *Give and Take*, suggests that somewhere between givers and takers there are also matchers. Matchers count the cost of everything. They strive for equal and fair exchanges with others. Their mindset is one of quid pro quo; if you do something for me, then I will do something of comparative value for you.

How people make business referrals provides a powerful

example of givers, takers and matchers. A giver constantly refers clients to other trusted advisors. A taker is always happy to receive a business referral, but won't make any themselves. Then, a matcher will make a client referral, but will expect a referral in return. In fact, some matchers will want to gain your reassurance and promise that you will pass them work before they will pass any to you.

People are drawn to givers. Those who are generous with their time, knowledge and resources are attractive and magnetic people. They are popular and help to make the world go round. On the flip side, we can all think of the takers in our lives – those people who only get in touch when they want something. Whilst we may all like to eliminate these people from our lives, it's not always possible, so we have to carefully manage them instead.

The fourth dimension of personal impact is whether you are one of life's givers or one of life's takers. Clients like trusted advisors who are generous in ways that cost them very little. Their giving isn't restricted to business transactions either. Givers will offer to help a client's child who needs career advice; they'll provide a sounding board for a colleague who has a difficult decision to make and will take time to check up on a colleague or client who had a difficult meeting. It might only cost a coffee or a phone call, but the impact it makes will cement a foundation of trust that will help you reap much greater rewards in the long run.

Dimension 5: Vulnerable or Invincible

I was recently moderating a discussion panel at an international economic forum being hosted in the United States. The panel consisted of some very impressive people who were each doing something incredible to make a difference in the world. I was impressed and could see that the audience were as well. However, I wanted more than that. What I really wanted to see was a human connection between the panel and the audience, so I took the discussion in a slightly different direction. I asked each of the panelists what filled them with fear or caused them to look backwards. They were incredibly courageous in the vulnerability of their responses and it changed the dynamic in the room from respecting what they did to admiring who they were.

It is a common marketplace mistake to think that professionalism and excellence means being able to project an image that your life is perfect and that you are completely in control. The truth is that clients think the trusted advisors who present themselves in this way are either in denial or, worse, dishonest. By being vulnerable with someone, you are effectively saying, 'I trust you and I want you to trust me, too.'

The fifth dimension of personal impact is whether you express your human vulnerability or project superhuman invincibility. Clients struggle to relate to trusted advisors who attempt to be invincible and inhuman. In reality, they connect to people who are like them – simply human.

Personal Impact

So, the learned behaviours that increase our personal impact on our relational ecosystem are very much the soft skills of relationships. Describing them as soft skills is rather misleading because it gives the impression that they are somehow less important and less business-like than hard skills. This misconception fundamentally flows against the essence of this book. Soft skills are the new hard skills.

A recent *A Minute With Matt* guest put it so well when they said, "Being heard is so close to being loved that most people can't tell the difference." Personal impact is determined by a cluster of behaviours that we either have naturally or that we can learn and enhance.

Key 9. Recover From Setbacks Faster

Early on in my career, I was trying to get going in the financial services sector and agreed to offer my services to a client without a charge. The plan was that my intervention would have such a great impact that the client would engage my services on a paid basis and refer me to others. Unfortunately, things didn't quite work out that way. Midway through the programme, the client undertook a review with the participants and it was deemed that I was wasting my time and theirs. So that was the end of that.

Inside, I was crushed. I beat myself up, saying that I couldn't even give my services away for free. I met up with a friend and explained what had happened and how I felt. After listening for some time, he encouraged me to 'fail forwards' – in other words, to learn from what had gone wrong and come back stronger. It was a huge battle in my mind and I had to make a conscious decision to stop beating myself up and become convinced that I could learn from this and become much better at what I did as a result.

When things go wrong within our relational ecosystem, whether a difficult client meeting, losing an important pitch or making a professional mistake, we find out a lot about ourselves and how resilient we are. Our resilience is based on a combination of our mental toughness and our learning posture, which together determine our ability to recover quickly from a setback and come back stronger. There are four possible responses to a setback:

Response 1: Resilience

German philosopher Friedrich Nietzsche said, "That which does not kill us, makes us stronger." Personally, I prefer to say, "What doesn't kill us has the potential to make us stronger", because whether a bad experience makes us stronger or not is dependent on how we decide to respond. Will we choose to learn from the mistakes and unfortunate outcomes and then keep on keeping on?

We have very limited control over what happens to us in life, but we have absolute control over how we respond. As success guru Tony Robbins explains, "Know that it's your decisions, and not your conditions, that determine your destiny."

Being resilient means being both mentally tough and having a commitment to lifelong learning. Resilience requires an attitude of never giving up and also an attitude that is hungry to continuously improve to get a different result next time. This is at the heart of what it means to be resilient.

Response 2: Give Up

Setbacks can cause some people to give up. We can resign ourselves to the fact that we'll never be promoted, never win the big contract or never build a successful business. People can write themselves off and believe they've reached their peak of achievement. In doing so, they end up settling for what they know they can do.

The truth is, successful people have been turned down for promotion, have lost contracts and have led failed businesses, but they have also chosen not to give up. The difference between success and failure is the ability to get up and start again, combined with an ability to look inside ourselves and ask, 'What went wrong?', 'What can I learn?' and 'What can I do differently next time?'

When people internally resign themselves and give up, they can end up spiralling into a negative frame of mind in which they feel low, experience mild depression and even mental illness. The deeper someone spirals downwards, the more of a challenge it is for them to turn their situation around and develop the mental strength they need to learn from what has happened and come back stronger.

Response 3: Learn More

Lifelong learning is one of the most important disciplines of a leader. As J F Kennedy once said, "Leadership and learning are indispensable to each other."

As an ancient proverb states, 'There is no end to learning.' It is, however, important to know how you are going to use what you learn on the journey. The pursuit of head knowledge without the resolve to do something with it, is folly. We can learn, learn, learn, but if we don't also have the commitment to apply that learning, we will never produce results and will continue in a pointless cycle of knowledge acquisition.

Response 4: Keep Going

Endurance and never giving up is another important discipline of a leader. As Napoleon Bonaparte once said, "The first virtue of a soldier is endurance of fatigue." Leadership is a marathon rather than a sprint. It is no good just sprinting when people are watching; leadership is about enduring day after day after day.

None of us should persist with something that is never going to work. Doing the same thing over and over again and expecting a different result is foolishness. So, having commitment alone is not enough in the pursuit of success.

Resilience is more than having mental toughness alone or committing to lifelong learning; it is the combination of the two. Mental toughness and lifelong learning together form the two legs you need to run a marathon. Without one, the other simply wouldn't work. Instead, they work in unison in order to complete the race. Let's take a longer look at how we can develop greater mental toughness.

Mental Toughness

If you are genuinely focused on trying to grow your business, you are guaranteed to experience some setbacks and even the occasional metaphorical 'slap in the face'. Over the years, I've adopted ten mental fitness techniques to help turn these inevitable stumbling blocks into opportunities. These are not theories, but rather practices I have learned from others and then adapted so that they work for me. I would encourage you to do the same; take them and make them your own.

Technique 1: Rhetoric

The way we speak to ourselves seriously impacts our performance. Negative self-speak can become a self-fulfilling prophecy that self-sabotages what we are trying to achieve. Instead, choose to use transformational language to describe how you are feeling. Use bigger and more positive words to affirm yourself and use smaller and less powerful words to describe your negative emotions.

So, when you haven't won any new business for what seems too long, you can find yourself starting to think things like, 'I always lose pitches' or 'I never win new business'. Transformational language would stop using negative words and say things like, 'I sometimes lose pitches, but I know I win more than I lose' or 'It's a numbers game and, from experience, I know I win one out of five pitches.'

Technique 2: Reframe

When the going gets tough, sometimes what we need most is to choose to see things differently. I ask myself the double-barrelled question, 'What is the worst that could happen and what is the best that could happen?' When I've genuinely worked this question through, I've normally found that the worst that could happen isn't normally very bad, but the best that could happen really is pretty attractive and compelling.

So, when you are facing a business opportunity that looks challenging, stop for a moment and ask yourself the same double-barrelled question. Consider what the worst possible outcome could be and what the best possible outcome could be, and then have a go.

Technique 3: Replay

When preparing himself for an important shot, the golfer Tiger Woods would famously remind himself of a 'moment of brilliance' when he played a particularly good shot. I like to play squash and if before a match I start recalling a game I lost, it's more likely I'll lose the game I am walking into. However, if I can remember a game when I played out of my skin, I'll be more likely to win the game I am about to play.

As such, the next time you make a telephone call to try to secure an initial meeting, pitch a proposal to a prospective client or prepare yourself for a critical meeting, replay to yourself the last time you did it really, really well. Replay your success in full multicolour, remembering the experience using all your senses of sight, sound, smell, taste and feelings, and then step into your new opportunity and do it again, perhaps even better.

Technique 4: Remind

A positive and expansive self-concept can create a springboard for your performance, achievement and success, whereas a negative or limited self-concept will create a glass ceiling preventing you from moving onwards and upwards. So, see yourself in the best possible light; as a person who is learning, growing and achieving.

Next time you start doubting or beating yourself up, stop and remember your value. Remind yourself of what matters the most to you. Remind yourself of your family and friends. Remind yourself of all that you have already achieved. Remind yourself why you got the job or opportunity in the first place. Remind yourself of all the people that have achieved what you want to achieve and that if they can do it, so can you. Remind yourself of what the best possible version of you looks like.

Technique 5: Reimagine

On a number of occasions, I've been asked, "If you could do anything in the world, what would you do?" Now, I don't wait to be asked. I regularly ask myself the question and reimagine the future. This is often enough to get the creative juices going without getting stuck into whether it's possible or not. By creating an 'if' scenario, you can help yourself and those you work with to suspend their self-limiting beliefs. You will find that as individuals begin to talk about their plans and ambitions, their aspiration and self-belief begins to rise.

Once the energy is flowing, a follow-up question can be, "If you were to take a step towards that future today, what would you do?" This can begin to tease out a plan, which, if actioned every day, will build momentum towards your desired future.

I was recently working on a new product and I lost momentum on moving it forward; the longer I didn't do anything, the more I felt demotivated. So, I got myself going again by asking myself, "Well, I can't launch this product today, but what action could I take today to move me a step closer?"

Sometimes, it's the first steps or the next step that can be most difficult, but once momentum is created, energy flows.

Technique 6: Retreat

There are legendary stories about executives from global corporations who regularly retreat from the busyness of business life and work, to think, reflect and strategise.

A monastery is a place where silence and solitude are part of everyday life. Some monasteries live in total silence, whilst others practice long periods of silence during the day. When I last visited a monastery, it was the strangest experience eating a meal with two dozen other people in total silence. Initially, the silence felt uncomfortable, but once I got used to it I began to process things in my mind that I didn't normally have the time and space for.

So, schedule time in your diary to retreat. It could be a lunch hour, in which you step out of the office and find a quiet or quieter spot to think and reflect, or a whole day when you can take yourself away. One of the pieces of feedback I constantly hear from people in the financial services sector is that they don't have time to hear themselves think. You can be different by creating time to retreat.

Technique 7: Relationships

One of the elements in your life that has the greatest influence on your resilience is relationships, both personal and professional. Don't do life or business alone, even though it is tempting to think you can sort out challenges alone. Instead, reach out to others who can encourage, help and support you. It is all too easy to turn to ourselves when we are struggling, which can lead us to turn in on ourselves.

An academic paper, *A New Look at Social Support*, by Brooke Fenney and Nancy Collins, which was published in the *Personality and Social Psychology Review,* looked at relationships and the impact they have on well-being. It examined the various functions within a relationship – namely where we gain encouragement, support and guidance in times of success and where we gain comfort, moral guidance and support in times of adversity. It is this second function of your relationships that develops resilience to help you come back stronger from a setback.

The Mental Health Foundation report, *Relationships in the 21st Century: The Forgotten Foundation of Mental Health and Wellbeing,* says that, 'People who are more socially connected to family, friends, or their community are happier, physically healthier and live longer, with fewer mental health problems than people who are less well connected.' Relationships are the most important influence upon your resilience.

Poor well-being and mental health has a significant impact on business. The *Creating Mentally Healthy Workplaces* report explains that, '37% of employees reported having had to take time off work because of stress, low mood or poor mental health, 68% reported to having gone into work at some point when experiencing poor mental health.' Often, this poor well-being and mental health is triggered by poor and unhealthy relationships. Knowing how, and being willing to repair a relationship with a client or colleague is therefore critical to your resilience.

Repairing a damaged relationship begins by leaning into the relationship rather than walking away from it, regardless of where the blame lies. The problem is not someone else's; it's ours. You have to take personal responsibility for what has gone wrong and for putting it right. When things go wrong in a client relationship, they are never deliberate. The difficulty, issue or tension has been caused by accident, so it is always best to start resolving the problem by explaining that what has happened was not your intention.

Once you have taken ownership of the problem, it is time for an apology. You may well need to start the ball rolling and this may be reciprocated by the other party or it may not, but it is an essential step to move forward. Then, and only then, can forgiveness be offered and accepted. A relationship that has been through a bump is actually stronger and more resilient because you will have demonstrated a commitment to work through the challenges and will have learnt more about each other in the process.

Technique 8: Recreation

Recreation and staying active not only have physical health benefits, but they can benefit your mental health, too. Sometimes, this involves going to the gym or going for a run. On other occasions, it can be as simple as taking a break from the office and walking round the block for 10 minutes to clear your head before getting get back to work.

The German philosopher Friedrich Nietzsche once said, "All truly great thoughts are conceived while walking." A colleague and I call it 'kicking the leaves' because one autumn we stepped out of the office for a walk in a nearby park and literally kicked the leaves as we schemed and dreamed together. Whatever the season, you can 'kick the leaves'.

The Mental Health Foundation report, *Let's Get Physical*, explains that, 'Participation in regular physical activity can increase self-esteem and reduce stress and anxiety. Physical activity can help play a role in preventing mental health problems and improving the quality of life of those experiencing it. For example, there is an approximately 20–30% lower risk for depression and dementia, for adults participating in daily physical activity.'

So, if you want to become more resilient become more active.

Technique 9: Rest

I was recently talking to a colleague who had tragically lost his wife following a battle with cancer. As someone who worked long and hard, his confidants had advised him to be kind to himself. So instead of starting work at his usual 7.30am, he decided that for a season he would start at 9am, so he could sleep a little longer and have the space and time to rest and reflect.

I'm naturally an early bird; I like to rise early and get lots done. There was a season in my life when I was facing an ongoing situation that was extremely stressful. For a period of time, I stopped getting up at 6am in the morning (which is my habit and discipline) and decided to sleep until 7am. The additional rest gave me the strength I needed to get through that time in my life. It lasted for about six months and then I reverted to my 6am rise.

Rest doesn't have to be sleeping more by going to bed earlier or getting up later, it can involve taking a day off, taking a long weekend or going on holiday.

So, if you want to strengthen your resilience, remember that your rhythm of work and rest is a really important contributor.

Technique 10: Refreshment

As mentioned previously, I record a weekly video blog called *A Minute With Matt* in which I talk about someone I've met and what I've learnt from them about relationships. Rarely do I manage to record the sixty seconds first time; it normally requires a few takes and on a bad day a dozen or more. Sometimes, the takes get worse rather than better, and I notice that my throat is feeling dry. So, I take a break, grab a bottle of water and then come back to the filming and nail the take first time!

When we are busy, it's too easy to skip breakfast or lunch or forget to keep hydrated. It might sound obvious, but eating and drinking properly will increase your performance and resilience. So, if you want to be more resilient, keep yourself properly nourished, especially when you are under pressure and there is the temptation to skip a meal or forget about your fluids.

Lifelong Learning

Lifelong learning is the second of the two legs of resilience. There is normally a greater focus in the business world on this leg than there is on developing mental toughness, so I've focused on the latter. However, here are some of the lifelong learning habits I have found to be helpful:

- Use a journal to record what you are learning or wrestling with, as this can help you to self-reflect. It doesn't need to be daily, but rather when there is something you are learning.

- One to one meetings with a line manager, mentor, coach or friend who helps you to reflect on what's happening in your life and what you are learning from it.

- Mastermind a group of peers you can meet with, whether inside or outside your sector, to proactively share learning and collectively help one another troubleshoot challenges.

- Undertake innovative reading, such as audio books, whilst working out in the gym or travelling, or using book summary services to help you digest the main points of a book in less than 15 minutes.

These are lifelong learning habits that you can take responsibility for and which can complement those more formal programmes provided by your business.

Resilience

Resilience is not about filling your head with knowledge or blind endurance. Resilience has two legs that work together: enduring and learning, learning and enduring. Together, these legs will help you run the marathon of life and ensure that you never give up on anyone within your relational ecosystem.

Develop Your Relational Ecosystem

The third priority in building your relational ecosystem is to develop the relationships that you have created and maintained.

As I look back through my life, all the good things that have happened to me have been thanks to particular relationships. For example, I can remember sitting with someone who declared that I had a book in me. They called their publisher right then and there, and explained that they were with a young man who could write them a powerful book. They then passed the telephone to me! In that instant, the title and thrust of the book had crystallised in my mind.

The 'hidden job market' explains that two out of every three jobs are never advertised because they are offered to people already known by the employer. This reflects the career path of many individuals. Most jobs are never advertised, but found through individual contacts and connections. The recruitment industry encourages and supports candidates to look for work through their personal networks and relationships.

In the same way, two out of every three contracts, non-executive directorships and other opportunities are never advertised either. There is a phrase, which I find rather crass, that says, 'Your network determines your net worth.' Whilst this is rather a base way to define relationships, it is certainly true that the people you surround yourself with determine the opportunities that come your way.

So, if you are ambitious for career development and business growth, the most important step to take is to grow relationships with people in your ecosystem. It is these relationships that determine the quality and quantity of client opportunities.

The third and final section of this book will explore four keys that will enable you to develop deeper relationships and build a world-class business one relationship at a time.

Key 10. *Build Deeper Conversations and Relationships*

An executive of a top ten UK estate agent said to his gathered sales team, "Stop throwing the benefits grenade!" When you come across someone who you think could be a prospective client, it is all too easy to immediately jump into pitch mode and tell them about the benefits of your product or service. Having an elevator pitch for your business is wise, but it's foolish to play it prematurely before you know more precisely how it is relevant to your prospective client.

Client interactions are most effective when you focus on trying to understand your clients' deepest felt needs and wants. As Stephen Covey famously wrote in *The 7 Habits of Highly Effective People*, 'First seek to understand and then to be understood.' It is more important to get to grips with what your client needs than to offer your solution.

Speaking too much is a barrier to growing the relationships within your relational ecosystem. One of my life mottos is 'listen more than you speak', because you learn a lot more that way. Great communication is actually about understanding rather than being understood. Marketing is first about hearing your prospects and clients, and only then about what you might say to them. So, lean into conversations, but hold back from speaking by listening and asking the right questions.

The Gift of Listening

Listening is often taught as a skill that involves learning to maintain eye contact, mirror body language and ask open questions. Whilst these techniques and others can be very powerful, they can also feel rather contrived. I prefer to view listening as a gift given by one person to another. The gift of listening begins by being totally present in the moment, by emptying your mind of other distractions and giving 100 percent of your attention to the person you are with. People who constantly look over other people's shoulders to see if a more interesting or important guest has walked into the room are not genuinely listening.

Listening is fundamentally about being genuinely interested in the other person, which naturally invokes curious questions that encourage the person to talk. Someone once confessed that they didn't think they were a very interesting person. When engaging with clients, it really doesn't matter if you think you are interesting or not – that misses the point. What matters is whether you are genuinely interested in your client. It's far more important to be interested than interesting.

When you are interested in people and genuinely listen to them, it is amazing what they will tell you. I often find that the more senior an individual is, the less likely they are to be surrounded by people who are interested in them. With their increased status comes an increase in the demands on their time, knowledge and contacts. More people want something from them. My experience is that if you gain a person's confidence, show an interest in them, seek to genuinely understand them and ask the right questions, they will talk very openly and vulnerably.

Legislation

In recent years, the financial services sector in the UK has undergone a major overhaul due to changing government legislation, which has driven the industry to be much more focused on client engagement. According to the Financial Services Authority, the Retail Distribution Reform is a customer protection strategy to establish a 'resilient, effective and attractive retail investment market that consumers can have confidence in and trust'. In essence, financial advisors now need to build stronger client relationships in order to earn fees for their professional advice rather than commission through simply selling products.

Similar legislation is now being implemented in countries like South Africa where the entire industry will transition to a model in which financial advisors will have to build stronger engagement and relationships with their clients. As in the UK, this will move the sector away from transactional selling, so the focus will shift to the non-transactional dimensions of client relationships. So, increasing engagement is now mission critical for the financial services sector.

There are five domains of client engagement that help frame conversations and build relationships. No domain is better than another, so I prefer not to think about them as levels, but rather spokes of a wheel. There is, however, a natural sequence to the domains and they flow into and out of each other. There are no hard and fast boundaries that separate the domains, but rather a flow of conversational energy and life.

Domain 1: Frivolity

The first domain of conversation is frivolity, which, despite its name, is not meaningless but critically important. Frivolity or small talk serves a very important purpose: it enables two or more people to feel completely comfortable and at ease with one another.

Have you ever been in one of those situations with someone you don't know or hardly know and there is silence? When you are with someone you know well, you can sit together quite comfortably without saying a word, but it often feels rather awkward and uncomfortable with a total stranger, which is why small talk is so important.

The topic of conversation is nearly always irrelevant, which is why I can call this domain of conversation frivolity. It is, however, one of those cultural rituals of social etiquette. Sometimes it's easier than others, as you can ask, 'What do you do?', 'How do you know the host?' or 'Where is home?'. If you are lacking any conversational hooks, there are the traditional subjects such as the British weather, the national sport, children and holidays.

I remember leaving an event in central London and making small talk with a lady who was collecting her coat from the cloakroom at the same time as me. We chatted as we walked to the nearby train station together and it turned out that she was the wife of the Metropolitan Police Commissioner, who I had met at another event. She revealed that she knew who my family was because her husband had shown her our Christmas card! It's amazing who you meet and what connection might begin as the result of frivolous conversation.

Domain 2: Familiarity

Professor Stanley Milgram, famed for his work on the 'small world phenomenon', wrote a paper called *The Familiar Stranger: An Aspect of Urban Anonymity*, in which he first identified the concept of the familiar stranger. Milgram explained that a familiar stranger is an individual who is recognised by another person, because they regularly share a common physical space such as a walk to work, a train station platform or a restaurant. Familiar strangers are closer than complete strangers, but have never verbally interacted with one another. So, familiarity can actually be visual as well as verbal. Milgram's experiments showed that 89 percent of people know a familiar stranger, who when spoken to would treat them in a familiar way.

When you know a person a little and something about them, you can move into the second domain of conversation, known as familiarity. The key feature of this domain is that you can pick up conversation where you left off. The more interactions over a longer period of time, the more familiar you can become with a person.

Picking up where you left off in conversation becomes easiest when you have discovered one or more shared common interests. These become reference points that you can always start with or return to in conversation. This creates a genuine sense of rapport, understanding and connectivity in client relationships.

Domain 3: Factual

The third domain of conversation is factual. As you get to know someone, and certainly as you explore working together, there are a lot of things to understand about them and their business.

Businessman and author Harvey MacKay explains that the most important thing in business is to know your client. As a young salesman, he developed a 66-question customer profile to help him understand his clients. The survey doesn't include any information about the business, but rather focuses on the client personally. It includes questions such as 'What are they like as human beings?', 'What are they proud of accomplishing?', 'What is their life like outside of the office?' and 'How do they want to be seen by others?' This profile has become known as the MacKay 66 and whilst it will be too rigid an approach for many, it clearly makes the point about the importance of getting to know clients at a personal level. It's important to remember that data protection legislation requires careful handling of the storage and use of any such information.

Depending on the service you offer, you could create a similar profile about your clients' businesses. This profile could include information about their leadership style, direct team, line manager, strategic plan, organisational structure, exit strategy and annual accounts.

At a minimum, these facts provide understanding, backdrop and context for a client's situation. At their best, they provide valuable intelligence and insight into a client's greatest needs and wants. This understanding and insight potentially provides you with competitive advantage because you know things that your competition do not.

Domain 4: Feelings

Talking about feelings is slightly uncomfortable for some people because of their personality, upbringing or life experience. I often work with private banks that help high net worth individuals and families to protect and grow their wealth. This industry is increasingly legislated and is particularly impacted by the 'Know Your Client' requirements to avoid mis-selling on the part of the trusted advisor and to avoid money laundering on the part of the client. Investment directors are now required not only to gather facts about their clients' financial affairs, but also to understand their hopes, fears, motivations, aspirations, aims and objectives.

Talking about feelings accelerates engagement and creates a much more powerful connection. If you are open and vulnerable to another person, you are basically saying to them, 'I trust you and I want you to trust me, too'. Openness is one level of trust, but vulnerability is a completely different league. Being vulnerable is letting someone into your world and revealing things that could actually do you harm. For some people, this is completely normal and for others this is a horrifying thought – if you feel this way, then please don't close this book just yet!

Domain 5: Faith

One evening, I was having dinner with a Bishop and we were discussing the domains of engagement. I explained the four domains I have described to you and he said, "There is a domain of engagement missing; there should be a fifth 'F' for faith." When we had finished laughing and joking, we realised that in a business context faith needn't have a religious meaning. It simply means putting your trust in another person. Faith is the point in a relationship when you decide to trust the other person with something significant.

The point of faith may be agreeing to let an investment director manage your hard-earned money. Equally, it could be allowing a consultant to come into your business and work with your executive team. It could also be giving a lawyer responsibility to restructure your personal and professional affairs. These are big decisions that, though you have done your due diligence, can also be described as leaps of faith. Whilst you may have seen the success these individuals have reaped for other organisations, there is no guarantee that this success can be replicated for your business.

Self-Orientation

It has been said that, 'boring people talk about themselves, gossips talk about others and conversationalists talk to you about you'. The best trusted advisors are conversationalists who help their clients to talk about themselves.

Only when you choose to be selfless rather than selfish will a client talk openly with you. This requires the trusted advisor to have low self-orientation – they have to be ready to shut up, ask the open questions and exercise the gift of listening. It is too easy to go into a client meeting with a pitch you want to make and key points you want to communicate, rather than to have a conversation that enables the client to talk about themselves, their teams and their organisations.

When you lower your self-orientation, it is amazing what people will tell you about their personal and professional life. There is clearly a moral obligation to treat what you are told in absolute confidence. The insights you gain will help you work out for yourself what that person's deepest felt needs are and whether your product or service could genuinely help them. If it is, then your proposition will feel like a natural flow of conversation rather than a pitch.

Profound Engagement

When you lower your self-orientation, you create the opportunity to grow your relational ecosystem. A big four professional service firm partner I coached explained that in each face-to-face interaction with a client, he looked to have profound engagement. The conversation could be about personal stuff outside of work, such as family and interests or professional matters such as leadership growth and career development, and organisational development about their business sustainability and growth. If these three dimensions can be set alongside the five domains of engagement, then a powerful matrix for growing engaging relationships can be created.

There is always a risk in business relationships that people settle for a degree of comfort rather than pushing through to another level of engagement. Whilst simply knowing the facts can sometimes be sufficient, more profound relationships are built when you enter the domain of feelings and invite clients to have faith in you.

Key 11. Work With Difference and Gain the Edge

The difference between good relationship builders and great relationship builders is their ability to read other people and regulate themselves to achieve the best possible outcome. This is what I call responsiveness – it's about having acute self-awareness and social awareness, together with the ability to adapt yourself to better fit other people. Some people have described this as emotional intelligence, mirroring or mindfulness, but I prefer to simply call it responsiveness.

Responsiveness is about lowering your self-orientation and/or increasing your response to others. It's about being empathetic, stepping into someone else's shoes and seeing both yourself and the world from their perspective. It improves your engagement, communication, impact, trust and influence within your relational ecosystem, all of which I have covered in this book.

People who are not responsive limit the bandwidth of clients they can work with. It's easy to build relationships with people like you. However, the real test of your Relationology is your ability to build relationships with people unlike you. Trusted advisors who are high in responsiveness have the ability to develop client relationships with people who are very much unlike them, therefore increasing their diverse relationships.

There are numerous frameworks that can help you grow in self and social understanding. Of course, I want to approach this from a relationship perspective, so I've designed a 'relational styles' framework that is profoundly practical and easily applied.

Precepts

Relational styles is a framework based on two precepts that are really important to understand in order to avoid misunderstanding and misuse.

The first precept is that the relational styles describe preferences not limitations. Having a preference for doing something one way does not mean you can't do it another way. A preference is not a limitation, but rather more it provides a natural default starting point.

If you were to take a pen and write your name at the top of a piece of paper and then swap the pen over to your other hand and write your name again, there will be some distinct differences in your approach that will give you an understanding about preference. When you wrote your name the first time, you would have done so naturally without even thinking – it was fast and effortless. However, when you wrote your name the second time, it would have been the opposite experience. You would have had to think a lot about it and it would have been slow and uncomfortable (unless, of course, you are ambidextrous).

The second precept is that no one relational style is superior to another. As you read this, you may be able to pick up on my own bias, but it shouldn't sway your own preference. It's a bit like reading two differing accounts of a political debate, one reported by a left-leaning journalist and the other by a right-leaning journalist. They are both reporting the same debate, but you will undoubtedly pick up a bias of the individual reporters. I shall do my best to avoid any conscious or unconscious bias on my part.

The relational styles framework is made up of four pairs of preferences, which I shall describe in turn. As I do so, you may feel an immediate affiliation to one relational style over the other. Please make a mental or physical note of this as you go.

Preference 1: Depth or Breadth

People generally have a preference for either building a few deep relationships or building a wide breadth of relationships.

I have a very good friend who says that he has a handful of friends – meaning literally five people that he has real meaningful relationships with. He definitely has a relational style preference for depth of relationships. He finds building relationships with lots of people unnatural and uncomfortable. In fact, he simply doesn't do it.

Another person I know seems to know everyone and many of them actually call her their 'friend'. She transitions between social settings one after another with complete ease. She definitely has a relational style preference for breadth in her relationships.

When working or trying to work with a client who has a preference for depth in relationships, it may feel as though they are keeping you at arm's length and not letting you close. Don't take it personally. They are simply a person with a few deep relationships, so it takes time for them to let people into their life.

Alternatively, when you are working with a client who has a preference for breadth in relationships, they may be very open and engaging. However, things might not progress quite as fast as you were expecting. Again, it isn't personal, they swiftly draw in everyone they meet and quickly form a relationship.

People with a depth preference are also described as introverts and those with a breadth preference are extroverts. It is a myth that one sits in the corner at a party and the other is the life and soul. Sometimes introverts are extremely good at small talk because they are better at asking questions and listening. By contrast, extroverts might flit around the party and appear to talk with everyone. It is sometimes very hard to spot the difference in social settings. The difference emerges afterwards because the introvert will feel exhausted and want to retreat, whilst the extrovert will feel energised and ready to go to the next party.

Preference 2: Left or Right

People generally have a preference in their relational interactions for logical left brain thinking or creative right brain energy. The way I remember the difference is that the 'l' in left is for logical and the 'r' in right is for cReative. This understanding was initially developed by the neuropsychologist and neurobiologist Professor Roger Wolcott Sperry. He received many awards during his lifetime, including the Nobel Prize in 1981 for his work on split brain theory.

Scientifically, this is known as brain lateralization, where there is the tendency for some neural functions or cognitive functions to be more dominant in one hemisphere of the brain than the other. The left hemisphere is about analytical thought, detail orientation, ordered sequencing, rational thought and cautious planning. The right hemisphere of the brain is about intuitive thought, holistic perception, random sequencing, emotional thoughts and impulsive adventure. The left hemisphere is logical and the right hemisphere is creative.

When working with a left brain dominant client, they will probably want to know the numbers and analytics on everything you do. By contrast, a right brain dominant client will want to know the big picture, but they will generally be uninterested in the detail.

Preference 3: Transactional or Non-Transactional

People generally have a preference in their relationships for being either transactional, whereby they are focused on getting down to business, or non-transactional, where they want to build trust and ensure people's feelings and needs are taken into consideration before they make a decision.

This is a relational style preference that can be particularly pronounced across different cultures. For example, in an Asian culture, a significant amount of time is taken to get to know one another and build trust before any business deal is considered. Business cards are also presented with both hands and should be received with both hands as a mark of respect for the position of the person presenting the card.

By contrast, in Western cultures, relationships can feel very transactional – you get to know people when you decide to work together and trust is built as you go. Business cards are handed out and often played with or left behind at the table.

When you work with a client who has a transactional preference in relationships, they will want to get straight down to business and engage in small talk later. Some people who are transactional relationship builders may even choose to avoid social settings because they don't see the point of them. A trusted advisor working with a client with a non-transactional preference in relationships will want to do a lot of trust building first. If having lunch together, you may not get onto talking business until the coffee arrives.

People with a preference for transactional relationships may also be described as project people. They are very task-orientated and will defer people matters until after the project has been completed. Contrastingly, people with a non-transactional preference are described as 'people people'. They are people-orientated and will delay projects and tasks if there are people issues that need dealing with.

Preference 4: Scheduled or Spontaneous

People have a preference for organising their life and relationships in either a scheduled or a spontaneous fashion. Scheduled people organise their diaries weeks and even months in advance. By comparison, spontaneous people may start a day or week with very little in their diary and fill it up as they go.

Perhaps one of clearest examples between scheduled and spontaneous people is how they plan and organise holidays. People with a scheduled preference are likely to be the early bird bookers who plan ahead to get the best prices, the best seats and the best hotels. Those with a spontaneous preference are likely to book lastminute.com, securing a bargain a few days before they travel from whatever options are remaining. They are inclined to turn up at a fine restaurant and hope to get a walk-in table or a cancellation.

When working with clients with a scheduled preference, you will need to pre-book appointments a significant distance in advance. Whereas when working with clients with a spontaneous preference, you will be able to telephone and say, "I'm in your area tomorrow and would love to pop in if you have time."

Self-Awareness

As I described, you will probably have felt an immediate affiliation to one of the preferences in each pair. If you are uncertain about one of your relational style preferences, you might like to ask someone who knows you well if they could give you their perspective.

As I emphasised at the start, the relational styles framework is about preferences not limitations, so resist putting yourself (or others) in a box. The relational styles offer you a tool to help you increase your self-awareness about how you naturally behave in relationships.

Social Awareness

More important than growing in understanding of your own relational style is gaining a greater understanding of the relational styles of the people around you. This provides you with the opportunity to be responsive to other people and adapt your relational style in order to build a stronger relationship with them.

My descriptions focus on changes you can choose to make in order to build greater client relationships. However, exactly the same approach can be used in all of your other relationships.

As we explored in Key 4: Leverage the Diversity Advantage, there are massive benefits to building a diverse and eclectic relational ecosystem. Responsiveness to differences in experience, personality and culture will enable you to build great relationships

Adapt

Adapting to other people isn't selling out on your genuineness and authenticity, it's about being empathetic, which means stepping into someone else's shoes and seeing the world from their perspective. Rick Brooks, formerly Managing Director of Equiom, a trust company business based in the Channel Islands, recently featured on *A Minute with Matt*. His point was that in order to be empathetic and step into someone else's shoes, you first need to take your own shoes off. To truly understand another person, it is necessary to suspend your own perspectives.

The approach I advocate to using relational styles is 'Acknowledge, Appreciate, Adapt'. The first step to growing great relationships is to 'Acknowledge' that the people in your relational ecosystem have different styles, temperaments and approaches. The next step is to 'Appreciate' the specific differences that exist between you and other people, because until you recognise and respect them you cannot work with them. The third step is to 'Adapt' – forego your personal preferences by adapting to someone else's.

The difference between good and great relationship builders is the ability to know other people's preferences and adapt yourself to achieve the best possible outcome.

Key 12. Grow Trust – the True Currency of Business

There has been an erosion of trust in Western society. The global financial crisis of 2008 has damaged people's trust in financial institutions. Child abuse by priests has created distrust in the Church. Institutional racism in policing has created distrust of the police. Phone tapping by the newspapers has caused society to be sceptical of the media. Unkept political promises have caused a fundamental distrust of politics and politicians. It seems that every institution in our society is at risk of running a significant trust deficit.

Trust is what makes business work. Chris du Toit, a partner in the African-based international private equity house, Multiply Group. Chris says that a business grows to the degree of trust that exists in its relationships and without trust a business will be impeded from growth.

Someone that I recently completed a piece of work for recommended me to a contact of theirs in another business. During an initial conversation about working together, the prospective client asked, "What constitutes trust?" The question caused me to pause before answering, because I realised I didn't understand trust as deeply as I could.

Qualifying and Differentiating Factors

There are two categories of trust, the first of which involves qualifying factors. These are the hygiene factors of trust that are required in order to do what you do. They are the fundamentals that your clients expect from you and your business services.

The second category of trust involves the differentiating factors. These are the factors that differentiate you and your business services from our competition; they are the dimensions that enable you to achieve trusted advisor status with a client relationship.

In my pursuit for a deeper understanding of trust, I have developed an acronym that helps me to both understand and also remember the different factors in building a trusting relationship.

T for Talent

The first T in T.R.U.S.T. is for Talent. This is the first qualifying factor and is about competency and the ability to do something really well.

The Gallup Organisation, who are perhaps best known for their opinion polling, are world leaders in understanding and developing talent and strengths. Gallup explains, 'A strength is the ability to consistently provide near-perfect performance in a specific activity. Talents are naturally recurring patterns of thought, feeling, or behaviour that can be productively applied.

Talents, knowledge, and skills -- along with the time spent (i.e., investment) practicing, developing your skills, and building your knowledge base -- combine to create your strengths.'

Your talents are the things that you find easy, that are virtually effortless and that you cannot help but do. When you are exercising your talent, you are being the best possible version of yourself and you are your most competent. Consequently, this is when you inspire other people's greatest level of trust.

Trusted advisors who are merely doing a job and offering a service that they have simply learnt to do will not achieve as much success as those who are operating in their area of talent and passion.

R for Reliability

The R in T.R.U.S.T. is for 'Reliability'. This is the second qualifying factor of trust that requires you to demonstrate consistency and to be a dependable person.

People who do what they say they are going to do, when they say they are going to do it, demonstrate the attributes required of high-performing individuals, teams and organisations. I must confess that I have a low tolerance for unreliability. If a colleague or supplier consistently fails to do what they say they will, when they say they are going to do it, I am quick to find a replacement who will.

It has taken me years of searching, but I now have a group of advisors for my own affairs who I know I can trust. In a large part, this is because I know they will do what they say they are going to do, when they say they are going to do it. It might sound like a basic foundation of business, but it is so liberating when you work with people you can rely on.

U for Upstanding

The U in T.R.U.S.T. is for 'Upstanding'. This third qualifying factor of trust is about character and doing the right thing.

Honesty and integrity are pretty basic requirements for anyone in business, but unfortunately these behaviours cannot always be taken for granted. We all want to be seen not only to be doing a good job, but to be doing it in the right way. It's relatively easy to present ourselves as that person when we are pitching to a client, applying for a job or undertaking our annual appraisal. A greater test of integrity, however, is what we do when no one is looking.

The best trusted advisors are transparent and always act in the interests of others and particularly their clients.

S for Synergy

The S in T.R.U.S.T. is for 'Synergy'. This first differentiating factor of trust is about chemistry and the ability to develop interpersonal rapport.

You will have a natural chemistry with some clients. There will always be those that you simply get on with and investing in the relationship with them feels easy.

Other client relationships might be a little clunky in the beginning and you have to work hard to develop a positive way of working with someone who is quite different to you. Now and again, but thankfully not very often, there might be a client you clash with and you will have to work very hard to win the relationship. If the relationship proves too challenging, it's often advisable to let another team member work with them.

The ability to develop synergy in client relationships is what distinguishes a great trusted advisor from an average trusted advisor. A good trusted advisor is good working with a client who is like them, but a great trusted advisor has the agility to work with people who are very different to themselves.

Synergy or responsiveness is something I looked at more extensively in Key 11. Work with Difference and Gain the Edge.

T for Thoughtfulness

The second T in T.R.U.S.T. is for 'Thoughtfulness'. This second differentiating factor of trust is about caring for people and not just about what they can do for you.

When giving a speech, I sometimes ask the audience to respond with a show of hands to the following question, "Who often receives an email or a telephone call from someone who doesn't want something from you?" The response is always consistent: a minority of people raise their hands.

I then turn the question around and ask, "Who often sends an email or makes a telephone call to someone when you don't want something from them?" I receive a similar show of hands. When someone we know takes the trouble to contact us simply to be thoughtful, it makes us feel valued and special and builds trust in the relationship.

This is one of the distinguishing features of a trusted advisor. We are all fundamentally a little selfish, so it takes effort to think about ourselves less and others more. Our ability to lower our self-orientation is an important factor in building powerful client relationships. It's a great skill to have the empathy that will enable you to step into the shoes of another person and understand the world from their perspective.

The best trusted advisors are like a great maître d' in a restaurant. They welcome the customer and make them feel at home and they take their order for their meal. Then, throughout the service, they are half a step ahead of the customer: they see when their customer's water or wine glass is approaching empty; they see when a course has been completed; and they anticipate when a customer might be ready for coffee or the bill. The best trusted advisors are thoughtful about their client's needs and wants, and anticipate without making assumptions.

Turning the Dial

Although we live in a digital world, relationships are analogue. It is not simply a case of trusting someone or not – there is a sliding scale when it comes to measuring levels of trust. There is always scope to turn the dial and improve the level of trust even if, like me, you give people the benefit of the doubt that they are basically trustworthy until they prove themselves otherwise.

One of the challenges of growing trusted advisor relationships is measuring success. Trust is complex rather than singular and so measuring it is not straightforward. One of the indicators of whether you have a trusted advisor client relationship is whether the client chooses to call you first when they have a challenge or an opportunity, and whether you can telephone each other out of hours in evenings and at weekends. These things are indicators that you have a trusting relationship.

Growing a relational ecosystem of people to whom you are a trusted advisor is about turning the dial rather than switching an on/off button. There are things that you do in client relationships that build trust and others that diminish trust. What are the things you need to do less and what are the things that you need to do more in order to incrementally increase the trust in your client relationships?

Your relational ecosystem is like a bank account. You need to invest in trust before you can make a withdrawal of trust. Just as with money, it is generally quicker and easier to spend trust than it is to gain and secure it. So, if you withdraw more trust that you invest, you will end up with a trust deficit and the inability to function in the marketplace. This can be applied at an institutional and individual level. Trust is fundamental in the world of professional services where expert advisors are hired to assist with the growth of a business.

Key 13. Get What You Want and Help Others Do the Same

If we are honest, most of us want to influence the people in our relational ecosystem so we can get something. This sounds rather Machiavellian, but is it really? A parent wants to influence their children to have good manners. A policeman wants to influence people to be good citizens. An environmentalist wants to influence people to reduce, reuse and recycle resources. Surely there is such a thing as appropriate influence?

Influence versus Manipulation

Defining and discerning the difference between influence and manipulation is not always easy.

Some scenarios are straightforward. An honest trusted advisor wants to help a person invest their savings in order to secure the best possible retirement income. By contrast, an unscrupulous trusted advisor wants to persuade a client to buy a particular financial product because there is a benefit in it for them. Regulation is part of the answer, but you can't regulate unscrupulous people out of any industry. There are many other scenarios where the difference between influence and manipulation is far from clear.

It seems to me that the difference between influence and manipulation is less about the techniques and methods used and more about the motivation and intent. Any technique or method can be used to either influence or to manipulate. I'd like to suggest that the moral litmus test involves asking the question, 'Who benefits?' If the answer is that only one party benefits to the detriment of the other, then it is likely that coercive manipulation has been used. If, however, both parties benefit, it is more likely that healthy influence has been exercised.

So, a trusted advisor who uses their skills and expertise to secure a transaction that benefits the client has used influence. In contrast, a trusted advisor who secures a contract that is not intended to deliver value for money for the client has been manipulative.

Leadership as Influence

Leadership used to be about authority, status and position, but in today's postmodern world, leadership is all about influence. Even in organisations where a command and control culture is still dominant, such as in the police or military, leadership through influence has become more important. In the new world, leadership is all about winning the trust and confidence of people to follow you where you want to go together. This is critically important with the service sector and in particular professional services, where it is all about expertise and advice.

Over the years, I have stumbled across and collected numerous techniques and approaches for influencing people. In this chapter, I am going to summarise ten of those techniques, which I describe as levers of influence.

Lever 1: Logic

Human logic is often where people begin the journey of trying to influence others. Logic is particularly relevant when the person or the people you want to influence have a preference for 'left brain' or logical thinking and activity. The more 'right brain' or creative a person is, the less impactful this level of influence is.

One approach that I've seen utilised time and again is to present three options along with the pros and cons of each approach. Two are extreme options, one overly conservative and the other overly risky. The middle option is then presented as the sensible approach with modest risk and maximum benefit.

The first lever for influencing a client is to make a case based on human logic that is neither overly cautious or overly risky.

Lever 2: Authority

In certain scenarios, authority remains a powerful influence on the behaviour of other people.

Authority is particularly influential when safety and security are concerned. It is also important in relation to legal and regulatory matters, such as the filing of annual accounts and VAT returns, where late payments can result in fines and damaged reputations.

Authority used to have much more standing within the general business community, but in today's zeitgeist, command and control cultures and positions of status are very much outdated. Many organisations have moved towards flatter structures, more egalitarian cultures and collaborative leadership approaches.

Having said that, people are still looking for individuals with the knowledge, experience and authority to lead. Being able to demonstrate that you have these credentials can help you to attract the attention of clients and persuade them to make decisions in your favour.

The second lever for client influence is the use of authority.

Lever 3: Scarcity

Scarcity is really the old-fashioned model of supply and demand. If something is in short supply and yet high demand, it becomes more valuable. Likewise, if there are numerous companies offering the same services as you and just a handful of clients who need them, the perception of its value decreases.

Scarcity is the basis of economic theory, which creates systems to manage the tension between finite supply resources with potentially unlimited demand. The thought that something might be running in short supply increases its value and desirability by others.

Airlines use this strategy when they advertise 'only three seats remaining' or hotels when they say 'only two rooms remaining at this price'.

These campaigns are built on research into the way that we, as humans, are influenced by scarcity of availability. This approach can be a helpful way to get clients to make a decision about attending an event, or to drum up interest in a new book. When time frames are attached to offers, people are forced to make a decision one way or another.

The third lever for influencing a client is the scarcity of an opportunity, whether there is limited supply of product or availability of time in order to ensure that they do not lose out.

Lever 4: Research

In the information age in which we live, research is not only a powerful means of influencing others, but it is increasingly required in order to attain, or retain credibility.

The Convention 2020 Research by the International Convention and Congress Association found that 76 percent of people attend events to meet people and build relationships. This statistical research can be used to influence the way conference organisers devise their timetables. Alongside orchestrating inspiring, insightful and impactful programme content, organisers also ensure there is structured and unstructured space for delegates to meet one another because that is their primary reason for attending.

The fourth lever of client influence is the use of research to provide insight and therefore increase the value of your professional services.

Lever 5: Reciprocity

Reciprocity is the human instinct whereby if someone does something for you, you will want to return the favour and do something for them of, at least, equal value.

Generally speaking, I hate the notion of networking because it is focused on purely 'getting' from other people. However, networking has a slightly more sophisticated cousin called 'business networking', which is based on the principle of reciprocity and has an explicit motivation of giving something in anticipation that you will gain something as a result. The foundation of successful business networking is trust and generosity. As you support others in building their businesses, you will develop the trust that will encourage others to reciprocate and also refer business to you.

The fifth lever for influencing clients is to be generous towards others because their human instinct will be to reciprocate and be generous in return.

Lever 6: Social Proof

Social proof is a psychological phenomenon whereby people adopt the actions of others out of a desire to do the right thing in any given situation. Social proof can be used to persuade people to do what most others or every other person is doing.

Social proof can also influence people negatively as it results in group think and herd mentality. It causes people to want to fit in socially, to conform to what is perceived as normal. Social proof can lead to poor decision-making, a lack of innovation and an inability to creatively solve problems, so it's important that you use this lever wisely.

If you are aware of the social norms within your area of business, you are in a position to guide your clients appropriately. For example, you can use social proof to encourage them to improve practices because that's what their competitors are doing, or you can use it to encourage them to take a lead on a particular issue within their field.

The sixth lever of client influence is demonstrating, by way of social proof, that many others are grasping the opportunity and they will miss out if they don't act.

Lever 7: Unconscious Assimilation

Unconscious assimilation explains that we become like those people we spend most frequent and meaningful time with. This process of influence is also known as osmosis – it is learning, changing and growing by incremental and gradual adoption and absorption.

Assimilation is what happens in a mentoring relationship. Coaching is a one-to-one personal and short-term development intervention focused on a particular need or opportunity. On the other hand, mentoring is long-term, even lifelong, and is therefore far more likely to be influential through unconscious assimilation.

Coaching and mentoring can be hugely effective ways for you to develop your relationship with your clients. Taking time out of your diary to invest in regular meetings will help you to understand their deepest needs and concerns, the way their organisation operates, and their personal fears and challenges. The more time you spend together, the more you will learn about each other and be included to work together.

The seventh lever for influencing clients is to invest frequent and meaningful time in your relationship with them because they will be shaped by osmosis.

Lever 8: Likability

Likability is fundamentally about having favour with other people. Likability isn't constituted of a single attribute, it is compiled of a multitude of qualities.

The cocktail of attributes and qualities that create likability include: warmth and friendliness to others, getting other people to talk about themselves and being able to walk in other people's shoes. There are also some things to avoid, like not taking yourself too seriously or being critical of others. Being able to have fun, laugh and joke, and also genuinely delighting in other people's success are also really important.

Likability is difficult to achieve, but the influence it creates is immense. The reason that likability is so powerful and influential is that we want to say yes to the people we like. It might sound rather trite, but the fact is that no one wants to work with someone they don't like. In Key 1, I wrote about how to work with people who you might not normally get along with. It's a key skill that will help to improve your likability and therefore your success in business.

The eighth lever of client influence is likability by becoming the sort of person that makes others feel good about themselves and who they would choose to spend more time around.

Lever 9: Genuine Vulnerability

Genuine vulnerability invites and invokes trust. If you are open and honest about something personal and sensitive, it is likely the person you are with will share something equally or more vulnerable. Transparency triggers a deeper and more profound exchange between two people. Being vulnerable is to say to a person, I trust you and I want you to trust me, too.

You are only being genuinely vulnerable if what you tell another person could be turned against you. So, telling someone about your children, your home improvement project or your hobby is openness, but it is not vulnerability. Vulnerability peals back the veneer of professionalism and gives someone a snapshot of what's going on behind the scenes of your public life. It is one of the great paradoxes of human nature that when we let down our guard, we can build stronger, more trusting and enduring relationships.

The ninth lever of client influence is to be genuinely vulnerable because it will often invoke an equally genuinely vulnerable response, which will build trust in your relationship.

Lever 10: Role Modelling

Role modelling is not optional when it comes to influencing people. The 19th-Century American academic and writer Ralph Waldo Emerson once said, "What you do speaks so loudly that I cannot hear what you say." Actions speak louder than words; people are far more likely to do something you show them than something you tell them. If you can demonstrate to a client that your approach works, they will be far more likely to adopt it.

Leadership styles are contingent on a number of factors. In a command and control culture, or in a crisis situation, a 'tell' style of leadership is required. By contrast, in a collaborative and co-creative culture, a 'show' style of leadership is required. The latter is far more influential within our current zeitgeist. As individuals, we all have very different learning styles and, for many, an ability to see and experience is a far more powerful way to absorb information than purely being told something.

The tenth lever for influencing clients is role modelling and leading by example, because people respond best to being shown rather than being told.

Second Nature

You are likely to already use some of the levers of influence I've described to influence the people in your relational ecosystem. Some of them you will use unconsciously, but by becoming aware of what you are doing, you can use them more effectively to grow relationships with clients. Others will be new to you and you may want to add them to the portfolio of techniques you use to influence people in order to grow your business.

Learning to influence clients, prospects and others takes practice. It's like learning to ride a bicycle, drive a car or sail a boat; you need to practise until it becomes second nature. When you do something for the first time, it can feel rather clunky and uncomfortable. Once you have gained experience, it begins to feel easy, comfortable and natural. The key to becoming more influential with your relational ecosystem is to practice using the levers of influence so that they become instinctive, learned behaviours.

Conclusion

There is nothing more enjoyable, meaningful and rewarding than making other people the centre of your world. The big message of this book is that if you want to achieve business growth, what will make the greatest difference is investing in your relational ecosystem.

It is important to remember that relationships not only shape your career advancement and business growth, but they are the greatest contributor to your happiness, health and longevity of life. Relationships are too important to leave to chance; you cannot afford to be lazy or even casual about relationships, as they make too much difference to you and your business.

Being intentional rather than accidental about relationships will transform your career and business. Lean into relationships by being more deliberate and less reactive. Commit yourself to creating, maintaining and developing a relational ecosystem that will transform your life, both personally and professionally.

Create Your Relational Ecosystem

You are comfortable about the task ahead because you do not feel overwhelmed by the number of people you don't know, you are simply focused on one person at a time. You can meet anyone you would like to meet through the people you already know by building out one relationship at a time. There is no need for you to resort to 'networking' or 'sales' behaviour that will put people off.

You can choose to develop a personal brand and thought leadership positioning so that you are known by your relational ecosystem as an expert in your subject. Then, when clients need someone with your expertise, you will always be at the forefront of their mind.

Human instinct builds relationships with people like yourself. However, you know the huge advantage of building a diverse relational ecosystem. Building relationships with people unlike you builds bridges to new thinking, possibilities, opportunities, markets and sectors. Unlikely relationships will create unlikely opportunities.

You are the only person standing in your way. Over-confidence repels people from wanting to know you and a lack of self-belief constantly causes you to count yourself out. You, however, believe in yourself and believe in others, and so have a healthy confidence about growing your relational ecosystem.

Whether you've been collecting relationships for years or you are starting today, keep going and never stop.

Maintain Your Relational Ecosystem

You know there is no need to try and sell what you do. People hate to be sold to, but they love to buy. Your focus should be on building genuine relationships with prospective clients, so you know them and they know you and what you do. When your clients and prospects need someone with your expertise, you'll be the first person they call. Similarly, when one of their contacts needs someone with your expertise, you'll be the first person they will refer.

You can't have the same relationship with everyone in your ecosystem. For your own personal sanity and professional sustainability, you are prioritising your relationships in order to make your world work. You are filtering your relationships with integrity. The majority of your time, energy and resources are focused on the people who enable you to pay your bills and make your life work. However, you deliberately keep some of yourself back for people who it appears can't do anything for you because it is the right thing to do. In addition, you don't always know who a person is, who they know or who they will become.

You know that your personal impact in relationships is not determined by what you say or what you do, but how you make other people feel. You are transforming your impact on other people by learning to see the world from their perspective.

Whilst you may have failed in relationships or other people have failed you in relationships, you have not given up. You are determined to learn from every setback and decide that every adversity will make you better rather than bitter.

Develop Your Relational Ecosystem

The quality of the opportunities you will experience in life are directly determined by the quality of the relationships you build. You have given up settling and making do in conversations and relationships. You are finding a way through the polite veneer and comfortable professionalism to a place of trusting vulnerability with your relational ecosystem. You are engaged in deeper listening, noticing what is really going on for people and then changing up the level of conversation appropriately.

You know the difference between good relationship builders and great relationship builders is the ability to read other people and regulate yourself. You are now stepping into other people's shoes, to see the world from their perspective, to understand their way of working. You are adapting your approach and becoming a more powerful relationship builder.

Trust and relationships are the true currency of business, so you are focused on building trust and gaining influence. Command and control, status and authority and failing to find value in this new world order. You know how to get what you want and help other people do the same by building trust and gaining influence.

Curating a relational ecosystem is your lifetime's work because there are always relationships to create, maintain and grow. The greatest contributor to your business growth and your life success is the quality of your relational ecosystem. Grow your business.

About the Author

Matt Bird is an international keynote speaker, masterclass facilitator and award-winning author. He has spoken in 30 countries to more than a million people. He has authored more than 10 books and he writes for *The Times* newspaper.

Matt is the founder of Relationology International, a unique approach to business growth through the power of relationships. Clients have included FTSE100 companies, big four professional services firms, private banks and luxury brands www.relationology.co.uk

The media magazine *Campaign* wrote, 'When Malcolm Gladwell sat at his typewriter and wrote the chapter on connectors in *The Tipping Point*, he must have just finished a slap-up lunch with Matt Bird.'

His philanthropic work building relational capital in communities has received commendations from successive British Governments, most recently for the Cinnamon Network.

Matt lives in Wimbledon, London, with his wife Esther, and their three children.